Educating Tomorrow's Valuable Citizen

Edited by
Joan N. Burstyn

Educating Tomorrow's Valuable Citizen

STATE UNIVERSITY OF NEW YORK PRESS

Production by Ruth Fisher
Marketing by Fran Keneston

Published by
State University of New York Press, Albany

For information, address the State University of New York Press,
State University Plaza, Albany, NY 12246

Library of Congress Cataloging-in-Publication Data
Educating tomorrow's valuable citizen / edited by Joan N. Burstyn.
    p. cm.
    Includes bibliographical references and index.
    ISBN 0-7914-2947-4 (hardcover : alk. paper). — ISBN 0-7914-2948-2
(pbk. : alk. paper)
    1. Civics—Study and teaching—United States. 2. Citizenship—
Study and teaching—United States. I. Burstyn, Joan N.
JK1759.E26 1996
323.6'07'073—dc20   95-36801
                                                              CIP

10 9 8 7 6 5 4 3 2 1

CONTENTS

v

Chapter 1

"What we call the beginning is often the end . . ."

"What we call the beginning
is often the end..."

T. S. Eliot, "Little Gidding"

Education has been the focus of an avid debate since the 1980s. Claims that the nation's public schools are inefficient range across many domains. In mathematics and science, schoolchildren in the United States do not achieve equivalently with those of other industrialized countries. Young adults enter the workforce lacking the skills to become efficient workers. Many teenagers use and abuse drugs and alcohol. Students are concerned only about themselves and not about others, and teachers and administrators cannot control violence in the schools. While many Americans are pleased with their local schools, they hold negative views about public education as a whole.

The authors of this book join the debate by raising a question implied by the issues above: what is the role of education in preparing people to become valuable members of society? Because the demands made upon citizens change as society changes, this question has to be raised afresh in each generation.

Several reports of the 1980s claimed that, to remain competitive in a global economy, the United States would have to provide new skills for its future workforce. We feel that people cannot gauge the effectiveness of education by focusing solely on its impact on the economy. We have taken a broad look at the way community is forged and the way it is maintained through the day-to-day commitment of its members. We have taken into account the diversity of people living in our society and our dedication as a nation to a goal of achieving equity for all. And we have considered the impact of fiber optic and satellite networks, computers, and video technologies on a growing understanding of the world as one society as well as our own nation as one.

The book begins with a series of questions asked by philosophers of education, James and Ellen Giarelli. Their experience of choosing a school for their daughter has led them to ask what we mean by educating for public life. Is there an alternative education for private life? What is the relationship between public and private schooling and education? Lastly, does the distinction we make between public and private education play off "more basic, perhaps pernicious, distinctions between public and private spheres, and

3

with that, gender-based hierarchies which valorize some lives while belittling others"?

Giarelli and Giarelli discuss these questions through an analysis of historical and contemporary literature. They use the arguments of R. Freeman Butts, who perceives several specific political values as central to the American polity and necessary for all citizens to understand, and Alisdair McIntyre, who believes that an educated public is impossible in modern society, as two limit positions among modern writers, in order to make problematic the phrase "public education." They then show how feminist scholarship has problematized the very distinction between public and private, and they end their chapter by raising the implications of these changes for discussions about public and private education.

In the new environment described by Giarelli and Giarelli, how do we define what we mean by a public? What relation does our definition bear to what it means to be a valuable citizen? Tom Mauhs-Pugh tackles those issues in the second chapter. He argues that "the good person must develop within a robust environment supportive of the integrated self," and that such a person becomes a valuable member of a particular public before he or she can become a valuable member of a broader society. Mauhs-Pugh uses arguments from the founders of the American republic to describe the circumstances in which the power of a central government may attenuate people's attachment to a local community. He suggests that such attenuation has indeed occurred over the years, and that, as a result, many people today grow up in communities (and schools) that do not provide the robust environment best able to help them develop into valuable citizens.

Is liberal democracy faced, then, with an insoluble dilemma? Is it impossible to reconcile the need for attachment to a small, and, as Mauhs-Pugh seems to suggest, preferably homogeneous local public, with the need for attachment to a larger society that values pluralism and equity, intervenes at all levels of society to maintain those values, and, in some cases, may undermine the development of particularized attachments? Fay Kelle takes up this challenge in the third chapter. She follows another path by arguing that we need to develop a new kind of democracy. She sees the need for all of us as citizens, whether we be students, teachers, business people, or officials, to "reclaim the public schools as critical sites for the struggle over and creation of a democratic participatory society." Democratic virtues and the practice of democracy are not, she claims, currently central to the education provided in schools in the United States. In fact, some critical and feminist theorists consider schools to be anti-democratic. Kelle is less pessimistic about schools. Hers is a vision of a society that supports transformative education in which schools enable students to learn to critique society, and not merely accept it as it is.

I think here of John Dewey's words: "the society of which the child is a member is, in the United States, a democratic and progressive society. The child must be educated for leadership as well as for obedience. He [and she] must have power of self-direction, and power of directing others, power of administration, ability to assume positions of responsibility. This necessity of educating for leadership is as great on the industrial as on the political side."[1] Kelle perceives a different need from the one put forward here by Dewey. He suggests that, because society is "democratic and progressive," all its members should have the opportunity, and learn the skills needed, to become leaders at some time. However, he does not suggest, at least in this context, that those who become leaders will choose to challenge the organization of society. Kelle does. The education she champions is one that is transformative; it provides students with the skills to critique what exists and to build a new and better society.

Zeus Yiamouyiannis has a similar vision. While he acknowledges his debt to John Dewey's ideas, he sees us facing different challenges from Dewey, because what it means to be a valuable citizen is changing, and because what we consider to be a valuable society is different from the valuable society of the industrial era during which Dewey wrote. Too often, claims Yiamouyiannis, education today is the transmission of the characteristics needed in the past by workers in industrial society. The skills of "collaboration, participation, initiative, expression, listening to and understanding many voices and many cultures, inherent to the emerging democratic, post-industrial society" are neglected. Yiamouyiannis's vision is for a society that encourages children to construct their own knowledge from an early age, that expects children as well as adults to "learn to communicate and receive knowledge," so that a true reciprocity exists in the learning process between child and adult. Like Kelle, Yiamouyiannis claims that a valuable citizen is a person who has learned to question what society expects, and who then contributes to a redefinition of those expectations in light of the conditions of the time.

The discussion may seem to have taken us into a future far from the day-to-day activities of teachers in schools. Not so. Barbara McEwan, in the following chapter, describes how a program called Judicious Discipline establishes a supportive environment for the practice of democratic principles in schools and a bridge between schools and society at large. Judicious Discipline is based on the knowledge and practice of the rights and responsibilities of citizens under the American Constitution, particularly the Bill of Rights. In discussing the program's implementation, McEwan paints a dismal picture of teachers' and administrators' lack of knowledge about the American constitution, its application to their work in schools, and the limitations it places upon their arbitrary authority. McEwan finds teachers reluctant to give up their authority even when invited to do so in order to teach children how to behave in a democratic manner. Nevertheless, when they do agree to do so, teachers and administrators appear pleased with the effects of Judicious Discipline in two domains: on the cognitive knowledge and on the behavior of their students. McEwan's chapter offers an intriguing glimpse into the difficulties of implementing change and the way the language of schooling differs from the language used by reformers. Judicious Discipline, by its very name, adopts a terminology familiar to school teachers and administrators. As a result, though its acceptance by school personnel is made more likely, its effect becomes less transformative. Therein lies a dilemma faced by all who would reform society's schools.

Judicious Discipline provides young people with the vocabulary of the Constitution to use in their everyday interactions with their peers, their teachers, their families, and their acquaintances. It thus provides a link between generations and a common vocabulary shared by the world outside the school. In his chapter, Donald Warren describes the historical antecedents of such education for democracy. He explains how fragile republican government appeared to the founders of American society, and how they, and those who followed them, believed an education in civic consciousness and political behavior was necessary if democratic government was to continue. Warren examines the discrepancies that have arisen in the last two centuries between rhetoric and reality: who has been excluded and why; how the methods employed in teaching democracy are often themselves undemocratic. In a truly democratic society, he suggests, one learns about democracy through one's encounters with all institutions, not merely the school; that, within the school, one learns about democracy from the organization and climate of the school, not merely from the curriculum, and from the whole curriculum, not merely from civics lessons. His chapter reminds the reader that the intention of civic education has been to produce not only good citizens, but also a good society.

What makes a good, or a decent, society? John Covaleskie grapples with this question. At the least, he argues, a decent society is one that does no unnecessary harm to any of its own members: "in a maximal sense, [a decent society] requires agreements about, among other things, the broad definitions of what constitutes 'harm'." For us to discuss such questions as, "What makes a decent society?" we need a social forum where different voices can be listened to, and engaged with, and where the contestation that may lead to a consensus can take place. Covaleskie suggests that "the schools might just serve as that forum." Covaleskie sounds a warning note by claiming that, if a society fails to shape children's character in ways that are socially desirable, it will, at a later stage in those children's lives, be faced with a stark choice: either to make them comply by force or to tolerate "the intolerable and the resultant unravelling of the social fabric."

A decent society is, by Covaleskie's definition, a compassionate society. A decent person is a compassionate person. Mary Stanley, examining the service experiences of college students, writes of the immediacy of compassion felt by a person when he or she develops, perhaps for the first time, a relationship with people less favored than him or herself. Such compassion, she suggests, may be quickly dispelled if it is not balanced by "an inquiry into the material basis of good lives and valued persons." Stanley examines the varied assumptions upon which service programs are based. She argues that in some cases, but by no means all, both the students in and the faculty who run such programs question the meaning given by society to ideas of justice and goodness, as well as the bases of economic, political, and social power. In our society, where "diversity will be the basis of whatever society the future holds," these issues are contested. Service programs, Stanley argues, provide an opportunity for students to reflect upon them.

In the last chapter, I consider what it means to be a valuable citizen in a society that values pluralism and equity but at the same time places greater demands on individuals than former generations faced. I explain how the demands grow out of new expectations of mental sophistication amplified by the new information technologies. In the environment created by satellite and fiber optic communications, the very terms "society" and "citizenship" become contested. New technologies create new complexities of social, political, and economic organization, in the same way that new ways of thinking about our lives create new complexities of individual development. Both these changes strain the democratic process and signal the emergence of new elites.

NOTES

1. John Dewey, *Moral Principles in Education* (New York: Philosophical Library, Inc., 1959), p. 10. [First published in 1909 as one of the Riverside Educational Monographs.]

James M. Giarelli
Ellen Giarelli

Chapter 2

✧

Educating for Public and Private Life: Beyond the False Dilemma*

*A shorter version of this chapter was published in Wendy Kohli, ed., *Critical Conversations in Philosophy of Education* (New York: Routledge, 1994).

Introduction

Although we both study educational theory for our livelihood, it was only when our daughter came of school age that we began to take the real-world problems of schooling seriously for the first time. As students of the public system from grade through graduate school, and strongly committed to ideals connecting democracy with public, universal schooling, we counted ourselves advocates for public education. However, as we examined the alternatives available for our daughter, a more complicated picture and set of choices emerged. In brief, this is what we discovered.

The public school system where we live in the suburban Northeast United States is widely considered a "good" school system. Cited as evidence are the high test scores students receive, graduation and college admission rates, special placement, honors, and individualized programs and curricula, marketability of graduates, and so forth. In brief, this system is considered "good" because it is thought to prepare children effectively with the skills, attitudes, and dispositions required for success in the workplace. This public school system is considered effective because it prepares children for successful individual competition in the private economy; in substance and aims, it is *private* schooling.

We wondered, then, where we might find what could be counted as public education? As we looked further, we identified a school, The Friends School, a private school operating roughly on the Quaker philosophy, whose aims and programs were more in accord with our own vision of public education. In this school, a premium is placed on non-differentiation into age, gender, or ability groups. Instead, teachers, students, parents, and interested community members struggle to work across lines of difference and hierarchy. The curriculum is school-wide, thematic, derived from discussion among those involved, and linked as much as possible to interests and as little as possible to measured ability. This school measures its effectiveness in terms of its ability to form communities of learning, relations of cooperation, dialogue, and engagement. This school's effectiveness is assessed against an ideal of full, free, communal sharing of knowledge, interests, and materials in service of associated development. In aims and substance, it is public education.

The contradictions, or at least problematics, present themselves. The public school, supported by local and state tax monies, takes as its purpose and standard the ideals of private education, while at least this private school, supported by tuition and philanthropy, takes as its purpose and standard the ideals of public education. Put more pointedly, the best "choice" for parents like us who are interested in their children receiving a public education is the private school, rather than the public, state-supported school.

One obvious implication is the economic. The Friends School, dependent upon tuition, is unavailable to the great majority of residents, including our family. And since the state, public school has little interest in what we consider public education, this means that a public education in any substantive, intentional sense is unavailable to most children.

While these economic questions are always important, what we drew from this lesson is the absolute necessity to problematize the language of public educational discourse, to look to consequences rather than causes and to assume that language, on its face, serves to cover more than it reveals. In this spirit of skepticism, in the remainder of our discussion we will put the very title of this chapter at issue. What might we mean by educating for public life? Is the alternative educating for private life? What place does schooling play in either of these possibilities? What is the relationship between public and private, schooling and education? What is the role of the state? Does the very language of public and private education play off more basic, perhaps pernicious, distinctions between public and private spheres, and with that, gender-based hierarchies that valorize some lives while belittling others?

We will take up these questions, not through an analytical, linguistic clarification of terms, although at times this could be helpful, but rather through a critical examination of historical and contemporary literature. One central problematic of the classical educational literature in the Western intellectual tradition has concerned ideas of schooling and education, public and private, so some of this material must be explored. In addition, more recently in the United States, a healthy debate has re-emerged around the aims of education, again centrally concerning the relationship between schooling and education and the alleged requirements of public and private life, the national and international marketplace, and the community of citizens. The 1980s featured important contributions to this debate, and some of this literature will be reviewed. Finally, we will return to our opening story, our choices as parents, the choices for our daughter, in the hope that this will open another, too long neglected, lens through which these issues can be examined.

Education and Schooling, Public and Private:
Voices from the Tradition

Much of the classical literature in the Western intellectual tradition concerns the aims and forms of educating for public life. Thus, Plato's arguments against democracy were part of an effort to provide a legitimation for a kind of social life in which individuals could find a meaningful place in a just polis.[1] For Plato, democracy, in its radical sense of rule by the many, violated the fundamental principle of justice by treating unequals equally. As we know, Plato believed humans fell into categories of competence and nature, therefore, for one to be able to do what one could do excellently, one had to do that for which one was best suited. Not all were suited to govern. For Plato, democracy accorded equal freedoms and rights to all desires, and thus equated the "higher" desires for reason and truth with the "lower" desires of the appetites and senses. Democracy, in his view, led to hedonism, a focus on the pleasures of the moment, instability, reckless change, and most importantly, disharmony. Thus, for Plato the aims of education were at once private and public, individual and social. Through differentiated opportunities geared to innate differences in capacity and temperament, education could both serve and harmonize individual souls and prepare citizens for the range of roles and classes necessary to preserve harmony in the state. For Plato, educating for public life was synonymous with educating by and for individual nature.

Where Plato responded to the instability of the life around him in the Greek city states, Rousseau responded to the decadence, stifling artificiality, and uniformity of eighteenth century European social conventions.[2] For Rousseau, democracy required a healing education which would return man—a word he used in a gender-specific sense—to his original nature and restore his self-reliance. Thus educated, men would then give up their dependence on institutions that had, under the guise of protection, ruled by taking away individual freedom and control. Rousseau presented Emile's education as the cultivation of the democratic personality. Rousseau tried to show that an "ordinary boy," Emile, could be the moral and intellectual equal of Plato's philosopher king, thus giving evidence for the possibility of democracy, albeit a democracy that excluded women from civic participation.

Like Plato, Rousseau links the public and the private, the state and the individual personality, through a particular form and substance of education. Unlike Plato, Rousseau does not see an innate harmony between the capacities of the individual and the requirements of the state. Rather, for Rousseau, the rottenness and malevolence of social institutions requires an education in self-reliance, self-love, and self-authorization. It is only after an intentional education apart from the norms, requirements, and foibles of public life that Emile begins to form specific, local attachments of love, marriage, and family which ground his activities as a citizen. In the end, Rousseau argues that education is a link between private and public—for Emile at any rate. However, the fundamentally different education of Sophie, Emile's mate, raises serious questions about Rousseau's understanding of the cultural meanings and valuations of the role of gender in educating for the public and private spheres. We will return to this issue later.

Like Plato and Rousseau, Dewey also sought some way to reconcile the seeming tensions of public and private, education and schooling. Unlike Plato and Rousseau, however, Dewey turned to consequences rather than causes as his source of meanings.[3] For Dewey, the distinction between the private and the public turns on an analysis of the spheres of perceived consequences of interaction, rather than on appeals to motives, human nature, or inherent qualities. When the consequences of an action are confined narrowly to those involved in the action, the action is private; when the consequences of an action affect a wider sphere than those directly involved, the action is public. Thus, for Dewey, individual action might be public, while social interaction might be private.

Dewey also extends this analysis to the formation of states: when actions have consequences that affect a wider sphere than those directly involved, there arises a need to regulate these consequences. Agencies and institutions are then created which eventually form a state. Thus, for Dewey, while a state agency, such as a public school, might be created in response to public concerns, its status and function as a public agency depends not so much on its origins or institutional role, but rather on an analysis of the consequences of the actions it promotes. Further, for Dewey, schooling is only one, and a minor one, among many of the institutions by which the social continuity of life through education occurs. While its special function is the transmission of that kind of modern knowledge stored in symbols, this in no way ensures that schools will be educative. Dewey reserves the term "education" for those interactions in which experience undergoes a qualitative transformation, where it is enlarged and expanded. Thus, it is equally as sensible to talk about schooling without education as it is education without schooling. And when joined to his analysis of public and private, Dewey gives us a straightforward way to discuss ways in which institutions of private schooling may result in public education, while institutions of public education may result in private schooling.

Of course, Dewey, like Plato and Rousseau, spent a lifetime developing a theory of education that would transcend these dualisms of public and private, and schooling and education. For most of his career, Dewey believed in the possibility of creating institutions like schools which could perform their special, largely conservative, task of transmitting symbolic information, within an environment in which these symbols, always in need of interpretation, could be the sources for the kinds of communicative activities that linked public and private consequences in the liberating transformation of experience.

These brief summaries are only suggestive of the many ways in which the relations of education and schooling to public and private ends have been at the center of the history of Western educational thought. Other representatives, such as Aristotle, Locke, and Vico, could be cited here. Instead, with this background, we will turn to more contemporary variants of the problem, some echoing these classical positions.

Educating for Public Life: Voices from the 1980s

As we entered the 1980s in the United States, with an administration coming into power committed to abolishing the Department of Education and with no record of thoughtful concern about public education in its agenda, some people felt it to be a time when those interested in educating for public life might just have to hunker down and try not to lose so much that there could be no recovery when, and if, things got better. As we look back, however, in the United States the 1980s turned out to be a time of vigorous, broad-based, public, sometimes even philosophical debate about education and schooling, the public and the private. While centered on some common concerns about the relationships among democracy, schooling, and the education of citizens, this debate also produced distinct positions. These views have been discussed elsewhere as alternative public philosophies of education, and analyzed in terms of thematic continuities and differences.[4] In this chapter, we return to the main varieties of the debates in the 1980s, with particular attention to alternate treatments of the relations between education and schooling for public and private life.

To frame this discussion, it might be useful to begin with a brief outline of the two limit positions. The first view, represented here in the work of R. Freeman Butts, holds that education for public life is conceptually and politically unproblematic and that there is a clear set of methods and materials available for its achievement. The second view, represented here in the work of Alasdair MacIntyre, holds that in the modern era the very idea of educating for public life is fundamentally confused, since there is not an educated public and cannot be one. Within the span bordered by these positions, a selection of views from the 1980s will be presented.

Limit Positions: R. Freeman Butts

In 1980, the noted educational historian R. Freeman Butts argued that the civic purpose of schools, their role in educating for public life, is their "most fundamental purpose." In *The Revival of Civic Learning: A Rationale for Citizenship Education* and *Teacher Education and the Revival of Civic Learning*,[5] Butts presents a conceptual foundation to ground this view and a set of detailed specific pedagogical practices by which it might be achieved.

In brief, Butts holds that "the goal of civic education for American schools is to deal with all students in such a way as to motivate them and enable them to play their parts as informed, responsible, committed, and effective members of a modern democratic political system. This . . . should include the three basic aspects; political values, political knowledge, and the skills of political participation needed for making deliberate choices among real alternatives."[6]

These basic aspects are elaborated further. Education in the skills of political participation will require greater use of pedagogical methods of debate, dialogue, community-based learning, and service. Mastery of political knowledge will require curricular treatment of the historically defined political community, the evolving constitutional heritage, and the character of governing offices and persons. At the core of all three aspects are consensually held civic values. Butts argues that "the fundamental ideas and values upon which our constitutional order is built should be the core of sustained and explicit study, based upon realistic and scholarly knowledge and searching criticism, carried on throughout the school years from kindergarten through high school. . . . I think that the educational profession, especially in schools and departments of education, should be trying much more rigorously and vigorously to become knowledgeable and explicit about the substantive concepts and ideas that form the common core of American citizenship."[7]

Butts devotes a great deal of attention to an argument for ten specific political values of central importance to American society. Five of these values: justice, equality, authority, participation, and personal obligation for the public good, concern the *unum*, the unitary tendencies, while five others: freedom, diversity, privacy, due process, and international human rights, support pluralism, the goals of *pluribus*.

For Butts, these core values define the American ethos, while political knowledge defines the essential features of constitutional democracy. While Butts is certainly aware that his decalogue of core values is the beginning, rather than the end, of civic debate, he has no fundamental doubts about the aims of education. For Butts, there is a foundation of consensually held communal beliefs and enabling institutions that bind American society into a community. The formation of an educated public requires that the community learn these beliefs and be initiated into these institutional practices. This is the fundamental purpose of public education and the fundamental role of public schools and teachers.

Limit Positions: Alasdair MacIntyre

In a 1985 lecture, "The Idea of an Educated Public," later published in 1987, Alasdair MacIntyre rejects this foundationalist perspective and offers a radically different historicist account.[8] "Teachers are the forlorn hope of the culture of Western modernity. . . . For the mission with which contemporary teachers are entrusted is both essential and impossible. It is impossible because the two major purposes which teachers are required to serve are, under the conditions of western modernity, mutually incompatible."[9]

For MacIntyre, these incompatible purposes are, first, the acculturative or communal, "to shape the young person so that he or she may fit into some social role and function," and second, the creative or individual, to teach "young persons how to think for themselves, how to acquire independence of mind, how to be enlightened." And these two purposes can be combined and fulfilled "only if the kind of social roles and occupations for which a given educational system is training the young are such that their exercise requires, or is at least compatible with, the possession of a general culture, mastery of which will enable each young person to think for himself or herself."[10] In MacIntyre's view, the culture of modernity forecloses the possibility of achieving these purposes. First, thinking, at least in the Enlightenment tradition, requires some notion of rational justification or rational objectivity. With no standards of rationality, there can be no coherent notion of independent thought or enlightenment. And with no agreement on what standards for rationality are, there is no possibility of providing a rational justification for initiation into or mastery of a particular culture.

For MacIntyre, "modernity excludes . . . the possibility of the existence of an educated public,"[11] and thus excludes the possibility of a justifiable system of public education in which the twin aims of socialization and individuation can be compatible.

MacIntyre's views on the conditions required for an educated public are worth considering in depth. First, an educated public requires a "tolerably large body of individuals, educated into both the habit and the opportunity of active rational debate . . . [who] must understand the questions being debated as having practical import for . . . their shared social existence. . . . And in their communication with one another . . . must recognize themselves as constituting a public."[12] Thus, an educated public is distinct from a class of professional specialists conversant only with each other and from a mass public which passively receives the terms and conclusions of the debates of others. Second, an educated public requires the existence of shared assent about the standards by which debate can be adjudicated; that is, assent about the forms and authority of rational justification. This shared assent must be different from the kind of skepticism that allows debate but prevents its resolution, as well as the kind of dogmatism that resolves debate by appeals to irrational or arational authority. Finally, an educated public requires "some large degree of shared background beliefs and attitudes, informed by the widespread reading of a canon body of texts."[13] For MacIntyre, this canon does not provide a "final court of appeal," but a tradition which must be treated with special seriousness and controverted only after special, serious argument. This textual tradition supplies the condition that distinguishes a mere reading public from an educated public, and mass literacy from public education.

Given these conditions, MacIntyre argues that the culture of modernity cannot sustain an educated public. In his view, professionalization and specialization in modern education militate against the creation of a large class of intellectually able citizens. The culture wars of the last two hundred years have destroyed the idea of a common textual and interpretative tradition, and most importantly, "the lack of resources possessed by our culture for securing rational agreement on what would be relevant and important for members of an educational public to share in the way of belief, in the way of perspective, in the way of debate. We possess in our culture too many different and incompatible modes of justification. We do not even have enough agreement to be able to arrive at a common mind about what it is we should be quarreling about."[14]

In this state of affairs, what can public schooling be about? For MacIntyre, public education without an educated public becomes a mechanism to promote private consumption. "Take away such a public with shared standards of justification, with a shared view of what the point of the society of which it is a nucleus is, with a shared ability to participate in common public debate, and you reduce the function of the liberal arts and sciences . . . to the provision of a series of passively received consumer products."[15]

MacIntyre is unrelenting in this analysis. In the culture of modernity, no amount of curricular reform, alternative preparation of teachers, increased options for school choice, or rededication of efforts can overcome the conditions that have destroyed the educated public and with it the possibility of educating for public life. As he writes, "the concept of an educated public has no way of taking a life in contemporary society. It is at most a ghost haunting our educational systems."[16]

Discussion of These Positions

In these last two views, we have the limit positions in our consideration of the questions surrounding educating for public life. Butts's view that there exists some identifiable set of beliefs, values, and institutions which provide a foundation from which educators can begin to develop curricula and methods for the educational initiation of the young into a public is directly countered by MacIntyre's historicist reading that these foundations have been irrevocably destroyed in a modernist culture and that, since there is no educated public, there is no possibility for a coherent, substantive sense of public education.

While Butts's view seems to make too little problematic, MacIntyre leaves us, as educators, with only forlorn hope. But forlorn hope, though desperate, is still hope, and even MacIntyre recognizes that the idea of an educated public, this ghost haunting our educational systems, is "none the less . . . a ghost that cannot be exorcised."[17] To struggle on in the face of what we know, MacIntyre writes, would require teachers to take up seriously the requirements of inventing or reinventing a kind of community that no longer exists. How can this kind of community be conceived? Where can we look for answers?

It is in the midst of such questions that the next section is framed. Specifically, we will consider three views from the 1980s that try to chart some course between the Scylla of Butts's sanguinity and the Charybdis of MacIntyre's forlornness. Robert Bellah, Richard Madsen, William Sullivan, Ann Swidler, and Steven Tipton, in *Habits of the Heart*,[18] E. D. Hirsch, in *Cultural Literacy*,[19] and Henry Giroux, in *Schooling and the Struggle for Public Life*,[20] all engage the problems attendant to educating for public life in cultures of modernity. In their views, we will find echoes of the responses to both the classical literature and the contemporary limiting positions.

Between Scylla and Charbydis: Robert Bellah, Richard
Madsen, William Sullivan, Ann Swidler, and Steven Tipton

In the last chapter of *The Public and Its Problems*, John Dewey
writes movingly about the relationship between community and
communication. For Dewey, the signs and symbols of our inherited
tradition, the ideas of public and private, freedom, rights, equality,
and fraternity, have lost their ties to concrete forms of associated
life and are thus powerless to affect public conduct. In Dewey's
view, a community needs communication, and the task of creating
new forms of shared life, what Dewey calls a Great Community,
requires new signs and symbols which reflect the social relations of
a metropolitan civilization. First among the outlived vocabulary of
the historical tradition is the language of the self, the private, what
Dewey calls the myth of the omnicompetent individual. Limited to
communication within a symbol system dominated by the myth of
the omnicompetent individual, the public is unable to make sense
of itself through public conversation, the public sphere devolves
into endless disputes among particular interests, and the forces of
the corporation fill the void. In response, Dewey urges the development of a new kind of knowing, a public science, a knowledge not
of the public, but rather by and for the public. This public knowledge will enable the public to understand and recognize itself as a
public and provide a system of signs and symbols whose meanings
are tied to existing forms of associated life. Within this vocabulary,
communication can transcend mere talk or the exchange of information and serve as the substance and method of public education.
For Dewey, this kind of public knowledge must begin in face-to-face
conversation, in the relations of everyday associated life, and cannot be expected from experts or agencies of the state. Democracy
begins in conversation.

Some sixty years later, Robert Bellah *et al.*, in *Habits of the
Heart*, take up the same questions: What are our "habits of the
heart," our "character," and how do we define ourselves and our
lives with others? What do our signs and symbols mean to us? Do
they give our lives meaning or fail it? At the core of the problem,
they, like Dewey, find an ideology of individualism whose pernicious effects threaten democracy, freedom, and the very idea of a
public community. Also like Dewey, they offer not so much a

philosophical analysis as a kind of public knowledge, which they call social science as public philosophy. In their inquiry, social science is wedded to normative concerns, with the aim, not of objective knowledge, but of telling a story of the characters, myths, and dramas that mark the sense contemporary Americans make of their own lives. And finally, like Dewey, they look not to the state or government, but to local associations and face-to-face institutions of relation—marriage, family, therapy, civic and voluntary associations—as the sources of these meanings.

However, while Dewey is primarily interested in reconstructing or inventing new meanings out of the tradition, Bellah *et al.* share some of MacIntyre's skepticism about modernity. While cognizant of the historical prejudices of earlier traditions, they wonder aloud if the only effective counterforce to a fragmented culture of possessive individualism is some version of a telic tradition, a tradition which could supply a vision of the meaning of life as a purposeful striving for some "Good," some higher, larger, more general, perhaps more objectifiable moral purpose.

What is important for our purposes is the contribution *Habits of the Heart* makes to the problem of educating for public life. Bellah *et al.* argue that educating for public life requires some notion of a shared, substantive, common good transcending private choices. Communication alone is not the answer; appeals to a received tradition are impossible. Some new form of integration, which they call a social ecology and discuss in terms of a culture of coherence and communities of memory, must be achieved through a social and educational movement. For Bellah *et al.* there *is* a paideia, a configuration of educational institutions that teaches an intellectually and morally intelligible way of life, but it persists too often apart from the "first language" interchanges of state institutions, such as schools, and the sphere of acceptable public discourse. It is in the "second language" discourse of wider associations that we encounter and employ traditions that *begin* with consensus, instead of free, isolated individuals, and thus start with some shared assent to the possibility of a common good.

These second languages, traditions of shared memory and purpose, can then serve as the starting points for public education. It is not enough to have one's tradition re-told in the first language of public discourse and become another item for consumption, enjoyment, or disparagement. For Bellah *et al.* it is essential that one's story be re-told in the language in which it was lived and through the practices that define its community or tradition. In this way, we all may enter a tradition, enter a world in which it is sensible to talk of a coherent public and a meaningful purpose for public education, not by initiation or induction through a canonical past, but rather through dialogue and association. In this way, we can show serious concern for the idea of the public, and provide access to a range of powerful public counterspheres of meaning to resist the privatized anomie of modern culture, while still rejecting the efforts of those such as Butts to ground public life in the abstractions of constitutional language and those such as MacIntyre to rule out the very possibility of an educated public.

Habits of the Heart poses important questions. Does educating for public life require some shared sense of the aims of public life? Does a serious consideration of the requirements of educating for public life demand an answer to what is arguably the oldest question in philosophy—Is there a "Good" and can it be taught? Is the idea of a "Good" required for a coherent, justifiable public education or inimical to it? The next view alleges that answers to these questions are unnecessary, and that a justifiable system of public education can be based on the fragmented culture of modernity itself.

Between Scylla and Charbydis: E. D. Hirsch

While Bellah and Dewey fret over the decline of a public and the loss of a civic community grounded in some sense of shared meanings, E. D. Hirsch, in *Cultural Literacy*, holds that a substantive sense of public education must be based on a view of literacy that is more than a technical facility at decoding symbols. For Hirsch, true literacy, the kind that enables communication, understanding, civic life, and the achievement of shared purposes, requires an initiation into knowledge of the background information, schemata, and taken-for-granted assumptions that give symbols their wider cultural and public meanings. Hirsch worries about declining test scores, but even more, he worries that the loss of a tradition of cultural literacy threatens democracy, civic institutions, the economy, ideals of equality, equal opportunity, social mobility, and the nation-state itself.

Hirsch offers a critique of modern educational theorists (erroneously lumping Rousseau and Dewey together) who have provided a rationale for a content-free, abstracted curriculum that encourages psychological development at the expense of knowledge acquisition and mastery. In contrast, Hirsch argues that "only by piling up specific, communally shared information can children learn to participate in complex cooperative activities with other members of the community,"[21] and that "the basic goal of education in a human community is acculturation, the transmission to children of the specific information shared by the adults of the group or polis."[22] Where Dewey held the chief aim of public education to be the forming and re-forming of publics, and that publics are *consequences* or *achievements* of communication, and where Bellah holds that the second languages of historical traditions and communities of memory might give normative grounding and substance to these communications, Hirsch believes there is a body of cultural knowledge, identifiable by the culturally educated, that everyone must know to be literate. For Hirsch, the primary purpose of public schools, their civic aim, is to transmit this information through direct instruction.

Hirsch offers a straightforward agenda for accomplishing this. First, panels of experts, such as textbook publishers and educators, will decide on the contents of the national vocabulary, the background information, and the specific fragments of the national culture into which the young need to be inducted. This specific cultural content, which Hirsch calls an extensive national curriculum, will be the stuff of public schooling. It will provide the schemata, what Hirsch calls in other places, stereotypes, forms of mental shorthand, and organizing tools, for processing the intensive curriculum of everyday experience through contexts of accepted cultural meaning. These items of cultural literacy will provide the categories by which experience can be encoded into habitual meanings that have been useful in the past; they will conserve the traditions of the civic community as expressed in the symbols of the educated cultural elite. Finally, general knowledge tests will be developed to assess the efficacy of such learning.

Hirsch's no-nonsense approach to the problem of educating for public life has had wide appeal. *Cultural Literacy* itself includes a preliminary list of "what literate Americans know," and several specific lists geared to different age and grade levels have appeared since its publication. For our purposes, the primary question concerns the tension in Hirsch's work between the descriptive and prescriptive.

For example, some may find in Hirsch an echo of Butts's position that there is a normative, political community; debate over its fundamental beliefs and values should ground the substance and aims of public education. However, Hirsch waffles on the normative status of his project. He writes that "cultural literacy is represented not by a *prescriptive* list of books, but rather by a *descriptive* list of the information actually possessed by literate Americans."[23] In another place, he argues that the tension between diversity and community, the one and the many, can only be resolved by a cultural division of labor. At one level, there is a need for a kind of civic religion, a value-laden set of beliefs about the normative purposes and ends of the public community. At another level is culture itself, directed by civil religion but in constant development of content through debate and intellectual exchange. And finally, there is a civic vocabulary, a value-neutral set of symbols and consensually held meanings that allows debate in the other two realms. Hirsch holds that his list of cultural literacy, value-neutral and descriptive, falls into this domain. Yet, in other places Hirsch is deeply conflicted over this issue. He quotes Plato approvingly that there are "good reasons for being concerned with the specific contents of schooling, one of them ethical: . . . whether a person is to be good or bad."[24] Hirsch writes of how cultural literacy places "higher value" on national than on local information and conceptual knowledge over practical knowledge. Unless Hirsch is committing some gross form of the naturalistic fallacy, deriving an "ought" from an "is" and thereby claiming that because there "is" shared cultural content, then we "ought" to induct the young into it, the reader has to conclude that his cultural fragments are both descriptive and prescriptive. His list of "what Americans know" can equally be labeled, for Hirsch, "what Americans ought to know." And while such prescriptivity may well be necessary, Hirsch's reluctance to provide a normative grounding for his prescriptions is a serious failure. In fact, the normative power of Hirsch's prescriptions lies in appeals to authority—the authority of experts, book publishers, the cultural elite, and ultimately, the nation-state. In the name of educating for public life, Hirsch would compel children to be inducted through the piling up of information into a prescriptive vocabulary and stereotypical schemata whose justification is no more than the coercive authority of compulsory, state schooling. And far from acting as a unifying or integrating force, Hirsch's attempt to compile an itemized list of cultural literacy *mirrors* the fragmentation of cultures of modernist, possessive individualism. Culture is not a list of items any more than a public is a list of individuals.

While Hirsch's view of educating for public life turns out to be a distorted, commercialized mechanism for authoritarian state schooling, he does raise, without answering, serious questions about authority and the "good." As he writes, "The question 'who is to say what the content shall be?' must not be allowed to serve its traditional role as a debate stopper."[25] Hirsch believes, and we agree, that his work "presents a broad challenge: to bring the hidden curriculum out in the open where it belongs and to make its contents the subject of democratic discussion."[26]

The next, and final, contemporary view on educating for public life we will consider, the work of Henry Giroux, takes up this challenge directly.

Between Scylla and Charbydis: Henry Giroux

Henry Giroux is committed to seeing that the question, "Who is to say what the content shall be?" is not a debate stopper. Like Hirsch, he is interested in bringing the hidden curriculum into the open and making its contents the subject of democratic discussion. Unlike Hirsch, Giroux does not back away from or vacillate about the central ethical decision that taking these interests seriously would entail. In *Schooling and the Struggle for Public Life*, Giroux suggests that if we take seriously the links among schooling, literacy, justice, and political democracy, then debates about public education must be explicitly normative and centered on the pursuit of a specific form of political community.

For Giroux, schools serve neither as vehicles of mechanical state solidarity nor as training grounds for consumer culture and corporate capitalism, but rather as contested terrains where the meaning of public and private, schooling and education, are constructed in the nexus of power, history, identity, and interests. Central to Giroux's view is the inevitability and educative potential of struggle and conflict, an active reconstruction in which public spheres are created and democracy and political community are reinvented. Citizenship is an achievement grounded in an historically informed agency situated both in discourses of critique and opposition and discourses of possibility and hope. Education for public life in a democracy must be distinguished both from state schooling and from functional preparation for competition in the private market economy. Thus, citizenship education cannot consist of the piling up of elite cultural knowledge or the initiation into a prescribed list of foundational ideas. Rather, education for public life "becomes a process of dialogue and commitment rooted in a fundamental belief in the possibility of public life and the development of forms of solidarity that allow people to reflect and organize in order to criticize and constrain the power of the state and to 'overthrow relations which inhibit and prevent the realization of humanity.' "[27] For Giroux, education for public democratic life requires the promotion of active agency which can critique and eliminate the "ideological and material conditions that promote various forms of subjugation, segregation, brutality, and marginalization, often expressed through social forms embodying racial, class, and sexist interests."[28]

Public education, in this view, as the empowering of counter-public spheres of resistance and public reinvention, focuses on strengthening the "horizontal ties between citizen and citizen,"[29] rather than the hierarchical relations between citizen and state, market, and cultural elite. In this view, public schools serve as alternative public spheres in which the borders that distinguish groups and individuals provide the educative occasions for the reconstruction and validation of authentic difference and enabling solidarity.

At the core of Giroux's work is the effort to address directly the imperative of prescriptivity while avoiding both relativism and authoritarianism. Is there a democratic form of authority, a way to talk of the common, public good without imposition, a way to advance a *particular* ethical and political view of democratic community and democratic public schools without indoctrination? Is there any way to avoid the imperative of prescriptivity?

For Giroux, the basis of authority through which educators structure classroom life is ultimately rooted in questions of ethics and power, since all educators have either an implicit or explicit

vision of who people should be and how they should act within the
context of a human community.

> I want to fashion a view of authority that legitimates schools
> as democratic, public spheres and teachers as transformative
> intellectuals who work toward a realization of their views of
> community, social justice, empowerment and social reform
> [and] ... to broaden the definition of authority and ethics to
> include and legitimate educational practice that links democ-
> racy, teaching, and political learning. ... [T]his task takes as
> its starting point the ethical intent of initiating students into
> a discourse and set of pedagogical practices that advance the
> role of democracy within the schools while addressing those
> instances of suffering and inequality that structure the daily
> lives of millions of people both in the U.S. and in other parts
> of the world.[30]

Theorists of public education express a continuum of views on
authority. Cultural conservatives, such as Hirsch, locate educational
authority in the unproblematic reproduction of dominant culture.
Liberal theorists also locate authority in tradition, although tradition itself is characteristically seen as conflicted, as in Butts's
decalogue of *pluribus* and *unum* political values and Bellah's appeal to the practices and memories of second languages that com-
pete with public speech for legitimacy. MacIntyre's deep pessimism
about the possibility of locating *any* source of public educational
authority in modernist culture is strongly echoed by many leftist or
critical educators who view all authority as authoritarian and thus
are unable to defend any notion of a public education.

In *Schooling and the Struggle for Public Life*, Giroux offers an
explicit alternative view of educational authority. Drawing from
the work of Kenneth D. Benne,[31] Giroux writes that authority can
be grounded in rules, expert knowledge, or the ethics of a democratic community. These alternative ways of grounding authority
form the basis of competing models of teaching, schooling, and
public education.

Rule-based authority depends ultimately on state power for
enforcement and thus supplies the logic for state education. In this
view, teachers are technicians of the state's ideological apparatus,
and educating for public life is, in practice, a functional prepara-

tion for the existing normative and political order. Authority based on expertise depends ultimately on epistemic claims, themselves deeply implicated in relations of power and interests. In this view, teachers are autonomous professionals, teaching is a service industry where knowledge is exchanged as a commodity to learners/ consumers for a fee in markets called schools. Educating for public life in this view either gives way to something called "choice," or is construed as effective preparation for a national and international consumer culture.

For Giroux, neither of these positions can sustain justifiable practices of democratic public education. In contrast, educational authority based in the morality of a democratic community depends ultimately on a critical public dialogue around two central questions: "What kind of society do educators want to live in?" and "What kinds of teachers and pedagogy can be both informed and legitimated by a view of authority that takes democracy and citizenship seriously?"[32] Emancipatory educational authority rests not on appeals to state power or epistemic privilege, but rather on the educational practices that encourage and allow "strong democracy," itself marked by a "citizenry educated by public thinking, political judgment and social action."[33]

In this view, teaching is a form of public, intellectual practice, legitimated not by its endorsement by the state or its claim to veridicality, but by bringing critical knowledge to bear in creating discussion of social freedom and public transformation. Teachers are neither state technicians nor autonomous professionals, but rather public educators. Educating for public life, while always grounded in the problematic contests and relations of real experience, is synonymous with schooling itself.

Overcoming the Tradition: Education, Gender, and Public Schooling

One aim of this chapter has been to problematize the question of educating for public life. As this brief review of views from the 1980s has shown, almost any agreement on a common vocabulary, set of starting points, or ends-in-view for a broader alternative is unavailable. Indeed, the fundamental terms of the question seem forever trapped in the hermeneutical circle. In the last section of this chapter, we return to the beginning story about our daughter's education as an opening into another, perhaps most central, problematic, the role of gender.

The last thirty years of research on, about, and for women has taught us that it is no longer acceptable in rigorous scholarship to talk of persons in the abstract, apart from their location. Thus, it is important to recall that the "child" in our opening story was a daughter, a young woman, a female. What does educating for public life mean for *her*?

Another element in that same scholarship on women has been a fundamental questioning of the concepts and categories around which male-dominated, academic disciplines have been constructed. Jane Roland Martin writes, "Since the early 1970s research has documented the ways in which such intellectual disciplines as history and psychology, literature and the fine arts, sociology and biology are biased according to sex. This work has revealed that on at least three counts the disciplines fall short of the ideal of epistemological equality for women: they exclude women from their subject matter, distort the female according to the male image of her, and deny value to characteristics the society considers feminine."[34] Political and educational theory have not escaped this indictment.

At the core of this feminist work within political and educational theory has been a reassessment of the ideas of the public and private, productive and reproductive, spheres. In her analysis of the classic statements of the Western political tradition, Jean Bethke Elshtain finds the public and the private as basic "guides to our orientation in the world."[35] For some political theorists, "the public and private recedes into the background of analysis ... because the existence of these spheres is simply assumed." Others hold "that the private should be integrated fully into an overarching public arena," while others call for the "privatization of the public realm with politics falling under its standards, ideals, and purposes," and still others call for a "rigid bifurcation between the two spheres with the private realm conceived instrumentally, treated as a necessary basis for public life but a less worthy form of human activity."[36] According to Elshtain, these ways of distinguishing the public and private are "unacceptable as the basis of the reconstructive idea,"[37] as part of the effort to recast "public and private boundaries to preserve each yet reach towards an ideal of social recon-struction."[38] Though reaching different conclusions, Clarke and Lange hold that "traditional political theory is sexist, not merely because women have been deemed to have an inferior nature or social role but, more importantly, because women have not been considered 'political animals' in the major theoretical models of political society."[39]

The suggestion that political theory and, for our particular purposes, educational theory, by focusing exclusively on received notions of the public is sexist is addressed in others forms by feminist philosophers of science and social scientists. For example, Sandra Harding describes how mainstream social science and sci-entific research are biased, not only by the fact that they have historically focused on men as subjects, but also, perhaps more importantly, by how they have assumed that men were "univer-sal" subjects and the public world, dominated by men, the "uni-versal" sphere of action. For Harding, this "falsely suggests that only those activities that men have found it important to study are the ones which constitute and shape social life. This leads us to ignore such crucial issues as how changes in the social prac-tices of reproduction, sexuality, and mothering have shaped the state, the economy, and other public institutions. Furthermore, this research focus does not encourage us to ask what have been the *meanings* of women's contributions to public life for *women*."[40] Marcia Millman and Rosabeth Moss Kanter note how this results in a systematic *epistemological* bias in social science research. "Sociology has focused on public, official, visible and/or dramatic role players and definitions of the situation; yet unofficial, sup-portive, less dramatic, private, and invisible spheres of social life and organization may be equally important.... When focusing only on 'official' actors and actions, sociology has set aside the equally important locations of private, supportive, informal, local social structures in which women participate most frequently. In consequence,... we fail to understand how social systems actu-ally function because we do not take into account ... the interplay between informal, interpersonal networks and the formal, official social structures."[41] Heidi I. Hartmann elaborates on this inter-play by viewing the family as a locus of struggle, as a *"location* where production and redistribution take place. As such, it is a location where people with different activities and interests often come into conflict with one another."[42]

This and much other scholarship clearly demonstrates how traditional distinctions and valorizations of public and private, the productive and reproductive, are enshrined in our political and social theory, and how these distinctions reflect and support gender-biased descriptions of the world and our possibilities for action within it. It is precisely for these reasons that "educating for public life" must be made problematic and looked at anew.

Jane Roland Martin offers an illuminating analysis of the classics in Western educational theory with special focus on the public role afforded to women and women's education in these theories. In much of this work, we find an oscillation between two extremes. The educational theories of Plato and Rousseau, though differing in their specific treatment of women's education, both systematically ignore the crucial issues of mothering, sexuality, and reproduction. While critical of this exclusion, prominent theorists of women's education offer a range of alternatives.

Mary Wollstonecraft's daughters are promised an equal access to education that encourages rational thought, and, through this, freedom from the enslavement to the passions that dictates the behavior of Rousseau's Sophie. Wollstonecraft also encourages women to preserve traditions of home and marriage. This view seeks the ultimate integration of public and private life based on ascribed gender-based social roles through the application of rational public education.

Catharine Beecher rejects Plato's gender-neutral Just State in her *Treatise on Domestic Economy*, and advocates movement toward an education of women for a separate and different sphere where gender predisposition is at the core and scientific methodology is applied to private life. By professionalizing "women's work" through the application of scientific procedures, Beecher hoped to demonstrate a way in which public and private could be integrated through a particular form of women's education.[43]

In a more dramatic case of divergent thinking, Charlotte Perkins Gilman created Herland, where the rich environment for learning is matched only by the fertility of its inhabitants. In *Herland*, private and public education are synonymous. Education occurs in the context of living, and the conspicuous presence of only

one gender enables the smooth integration of production and reproduction, public and private. In the paideia of Herland, "an exquis-
ite literature . . . permeates the atmosphere; the sciences—anatomy,
physiology, nutrition, botany, chemistry—are linked everywhere to
practice; history and psychology are closely bound up with each
other; physical and mental development are expected to take place
together"[44] with an overarching ideal of mother love. In one sense
this view seems to integrate the public and private through education as life, and life as education. However, unlike Rousseau's peri-
patetic Emile, who acquired a gender-specific half-wisdom,
Herlanders acquire a wisdom that is gender-denied.

In all these cases, we see the embrace of dichotomy. Plato
dichotomizes public and private roles. Rousseau separates by gender. Wollstonecraft embraces rational thought, but retains ascribed
social roles. Beecher would have women educated separately and
differently with a scientific model. Gilman would eliminate the
detail of gender. In contrast, Jane Roland Martin suggests a new
theory of educational practices that moves toward a reconstructive
ideal. For Martin, the fallacy of the false dilemma, education for
public *or* private life, education for productive *or* reproductive functions, education based on gender *or* education having nothing to do
with gender, "is a natural consequence of our ignorance of alternative ideals of the educated woman."[45] The proper construction of
educational theories, for men and women, requires that equal due
be given to the historically-defined productive realm—preparation
for citizenship and the workplace—*and* the reproductive realm, in
which Martin includes "not simply conception and birth, but the
rearing of children to more or less maturity and associated activities such as tending the sick, taking care of family needs, and
running a household."[46] In this view, educational theory might
still embrace dichotomy—not the simple one of gender or social
role, but that found in the complementary relationships formed
between people. These are as diverse and complex as the traits of
humankind.

What would inquiry into educating for public life become if we
seriously followed the idea that an educational theory was a theory
or theories of the "doings" that prepare one for conduct as a member of community? What would such inquiry become if we seriously
followed the idea that education itself is the paradigmatic mode of

socially established, cooperative human activity through which we attempt systematically to extend all varieties of human powers and excellences, and that these powers and excellences do not come neatly packaged in gender-driven categories of public and private, productive and reproductive?

An education for living in common would require us to acquire knowledge of self and other, to break from a tradition of divergence, and to integrate the merely conceptual domains of "public" and "private." We think a good beginning, a prolegomena to a curriculum of common sense, that we have used in conversation with students, is to engage in dialogue about what excellence means in common-sense terms, where we take common sense literally as the sense it takes to live in a commons. It quickly becomes clear that when we consider the people we respect, love, are glad to get to know and have as neighbors, work with, and so forth, we do not think of these people solely, if at all, in school-based categories of cognition and symbolic literacy or in theoretically-driven categories which distinguish between public and private. We know some people we would go to hear speak or for heart surgery, but not go hiking with or invite to our birthday parties. That is, we build our publics over a spectrum of competencies and qualities that people display in their lives and bring to ours. We operate publicly in terms of a system of multiple excellences about which we make sophisticated, finely-honed comparative judgments.[47] The ability to make these judgments, to bring the skill, know-how, know-that, empathy, and imagination to bear in re-creating a world, is a large part of what it means to be educated. In this process, the walls between public and private, productive and reproductive, are collapsed. That is, we see quickly how so-called public virtues and competencies such as efficiency and rationality are desiderata in some activities of the private world, while so-called private virtues and competencies such as nurturance and courage are requirements for an enabling and generous public life. If the aim of public education is educating for public life, forming and reforming publics, then the purpose of schooling is to prepare people in the multiple excellences that give a public its quality, distinctiveness, and solidarity. And it is in large part the discourses of the private, reproductive practices that give public discourse its substance and its possibilities for education.

Conclusion

Every distinction, and perhaps especially the distinction between private and public, and productive and reproductive, masks power and claims of privilege. Feminist scholarship has shown the distorting consequences that power and claims of privilege have had in theories of public education and has opened a lens on a reconstructive ideal in whose light our children, daughters and sons, may, in Dewey's terms, "learn to be human."[48]

NOTES

1. *The Republic of Plato*, translated by Francis W. Cornford (London: Oxford University Press, 1973).

2. Jean Jacques Rousseau, *Emile, or On Education*, introduction, translation, and notes by Allan Bloom (New York: Basic Books, 1979).

3. John Dewey, *Democracy and Education* (New York: Free Press, 1966), and *The Public and Its Problems* (New York: Henry Holt, 1927).

4. James M. Giarelli, "Public Philosophies and Education," *Educational Foundations* 4 (Winter 1990): 7–18.

5. R. Freeman Butts, *The Revival of Civic Learning: A Rationale for Citizenship Education in American Schools* (Bloomington, Ind.: Phi Delta Kappan Educational Foundation, 1980), and *Teacher Education and the Revival of Civic Learning*, Seventh Annual DeGarmo Lecture (Society of Professors of Education, 1982).

6. Butts, *Revival of Civic Learning*, p. 123.

7. Butts, *Teacher Education*, p. 14.

8. Alasdair MacIntyre, "The Idea of an Educated Public," in Graham Haydon, ed., *Education and Values* (London: Institute of Education, University of London, 1987).

9. *Ibid.*, p. 16.

10. *Ibid.*

11. *Ibid.*, p. 17.

12. *Ibid.*, p. 18.

13. *Ibid.*, p. 19.

14. *Ibid.*, p. 28.

15. *Ibid.*, p. 29.

16. *Ibid.*, p. 34.

17. *Ibid.*

18. Robert Bellah, Richard Madsen, William Sullivan, Ann Swidler, and Steven Tipton, *Habits of the Heart* (Berkeley: University of California Press, 1985).

19. E. D. Hirsch, *Cultural Literacy* (Boston: Houghton Mifflin, 1987).

20. Henry Giroux, *Schooling and the Struggle for Public Life* (Minneapolis: University of Minnesota Press, 1988.)

21. *Cultural Literacy*, p. xv.

22. *Ibid.*, p. xvi.

23. *Ibid.*, p. xiv.

24. *Ibid.*, p. xvi.

25. *Ibid.*, p. 144.

26. *Ibid.*, p. 145.

27. Giroux, *Schooling and the Struggle for Public Life*, p. 6. Giroux's internal quotation is from Douglas Kellner and Harry O'Hara, "Utopianism and Marxism in Ernst Bloch," *New German Critique* 9 (Fall 1976): 22.

28. *Ibid.*

29. *Ibid.*, p. 30.

30. *Ibid.*, pp. 72–3.

31. Kenneth D. Benne, "Authority in Education," *Harvard Educational Review* 40 (August 1970): 345–410.

32. Giroux, *Schooling and the Struggle for Public Life*, p. 88.

33. *Ibid.*

34. Jane Roland Martin, *Reclaiming a Conversation* (New Haven: Yale University Press, 1985), p. 3.

35. Jean Bethke Elshtain, *Public Man, Private Woman* (Princeton: Princeton University Press, 1981), p. 3.

36. *Ibid.*, p. 4.

37. *Ibid.*, p. 342.

38. *Ibid.*, p. 4.

39. Lorenne M.G. Clarke and Lynda Lange, eds., *The Sexism of Social and Political Theory* (Toronto: University of Toronto Press, 1979), p. vii.

40. Sandra Harding, ed., *Feminism and Methodology* (Bloomington, Ind.: Indiana University Press, 1987), pp. 4–5. Emphasis in original.

41. Marcia Millman and Rosabeth Moss Kanter, "Introduction to *Another Voice: Feminist Perspectives in Social Life and Social Science*," in Harding, ed., *Feminism and Methodology,* p. 32.

42. Heidi I. Hartmann, "The Family as the Locus of Gender, Class, and Political Struggle: The Example of Housework," in Harding, *Feminism and Methodology*, p. 111.

43. Further discussion of Beecher's views on the professionalization of women's work may be found in Kathryn Kish Sklar, *Catharine Beecher: A Study in American Domesticity* (New Haven, Conn.: Yale University Press, 1973), and Joan N. Burstyn, "Catharine Beecher and the Education of American Women," *New England Quarterly* 47, no. 3 (September 1974): 386–403.

44. Martin, *Reclaiming a Conversation,* pp. 147–48.

45. *Ibid.*, p. 176.

46. *Ibid.*, p. 6.

47. See Maxine Greene, "Excellence, Meanings, and Multiplicity," *Teachers College Record* 86 (1984): 283–97.

48. John Dewey, *The Public and Its Problems* (Chicago: Swallow Press, 1954), p. 154.

Thomas Mauhs-Pugh

Chapter 3

✧

Developing the Good Person:
The Role of Local Publics

Introduction

"Educating valuable citizens for tomorrow's society" lends itself to a multiplicity of interpretations. The task I have set myself is to lay out some necessary formal considerations of the relationship between education and the development of a "valuable" person within the context of any society, but specifically as a problem of developing personal integrity within a liberal democratic society.[1]

By speaking of a "valuable member" in relation to a society, I refer to a good person in a good society. Aristotle set a useful precedent in his *Politics* by clarifying "that it is possible to be a good citizen without possessing the excellence which is the quality of the good man [*sic*]."[2] In a modern context, we might envision the Nazi who was valued by other Nazis as a good citizen of Germany under a Nazi government. Thus, it is important that "valuable member" be modified by "valuable society." I do not raise the issue in order to argue about the possible meanings of "citizenship" or "valuable." I mention this point for two reasons.

First, I am interested in talking about people as internally integrated beings. I do not want to focus just on some role they assume which we might refer to as "citizen." By focusing merely on the idea of a citizen, we would subordinate the individual to the condition of being judged only in relation to his or her usefulness to a larger social aggregate, without providing evaluative criteria for the society.

Secondly, although I do not wish to argue here for a particular conception of the good society, I do wish to use "society" to represent a form of social frame which we may value. I suggest some parameters within which such a valued society might exist, while I remain relatively neutral to more particular formulations of the good. I do not argue for evaluative criteria by which we can identify and judge "bad" societies.

Nevertheless, I do assume that I and the reader share an understanding of the concepts of liberalism and democracy. Philosophic liberalism might be loosely characterized by an emphasis on individual freedom from the arbitrary exercise of power and by a concern for government by law under the authority and consent of the governed. The core of liberalism is a belief that individuals have rights. The notion of essential autonomy of the individual has a history of conflicting interpretations. Individual autonomy is problematic for liberalism and is not central to liberal philosophy *per se*.

Democracy might be characterized by a belief that citizens have the right and should have the opportunity to participate in government. The definitions of both liberalism and democracy are formal. They do not specify the content of any particular theory or manifestation of either liberalism or democracy. Neither "rights," nor "citizens," nor "participation" are defined.

My intent, here, is to provide a framework within which we can better understand some implications of contemporary educational reform movements in the United States. The nub of the argument is that good people, in general, develop only within the context of communities which themselves have robust and particular conceptions of what it means to be a good person. Though I have chosen not to explicate the specific content or structure of value of a given community, each community does value certain things to which a member of that community must be loyal in order for that person to be a member. So, one of the essential ingredients of being a valuable member is loyalty.[3]

The Argument

Andrew Oldenquist writes, "non-caring, and alienation . . . seem to be caused more by the absence of expected loyalties than by the absence of ordinary moral conscientiousness."[4] Oldenquist suggests that being morally conscientious in a specific instance or relation requires seeing oneself as somehow attached to something integral to that circumstance. Now, Oldenquist is careful to distinguish loyalty from attachment to an ideal. To have loyalty is to be attached to a particular thing, not just some kind of thing, and to come to see it as one's own, as "*mine*."[5] Seeing something as mine is not, however, exclusionary. Others may have the same object of loyalty. A commonality of loyalties is probably necessary, though not sufficient, to constitute a community.

Oldenquist goes on to argue that simply being mine is insufficient grounds for loyalty. The thing one is loyal to "must have features that make it worth having."[6] But being mine and valued are only minimum conditions. Loyalty varies in strength. To say one is loyal to one's family is not to preclude a conflicting loyalty. A person whose strongest loyalty is to his or her family may still not deny that a "family sacrifice can be outweighed when . . .

balanced against some great harm to be avoided (or good to be achieved) by his community or his country."[7]

The strength of specific loyalties is inverse to the distance of the object from the individual. Loyalty to family and friends is greater than loyalty to a city or state, which is greater than loyalty to a country, which is greater than loyalty to the United Nations or humanity in general. The strength of loyalty requires a feeling that *this* is mine; attachment to anything can be precluded by feelings of alienation. One might feel more loyal to one's country than to one's family, or more loyal to humanity than to one's country. However, such attachments indicate a problem. We generally assume alienation to indicate something amiss. What is wrong with me or my family or my country that I cannot feel greater loyalty to them? Most of us detest the Hitler Youth who informed on their parents, relations, and friends.

We desire a society and circumstances in which alienation and the conflict of loyalties are minimized. That desire, I submit, is strongest for those attachments we would expect to be the strongest and closest, i.e., family, friends, a community. Such localized and particular attachments, of course, present a problem to larger aggregates of humanity. A country composed of diverse communities may well fear dissolution or disabling antagonisms if individual and group loyalty cannot be sufficiently wedded to the nation. It was just such fear of dissolution that provided the impetus behind the move in our country to scrap the Articles of Confederation in favor of a Constitution that gave the Federal government more centralized power. Alexander Hamilton responded to complaints by the anti-federalists that the federal government would interfere too strongly in local affairs:

> It will always be far easier for the State governments to encroach upon the national authorities than for the national government to encroach upon the State authorities. . . . Upon the same principle that a man is more attached to his family than to his neighborhood, to his neighborhood than to the community at large, the people of each State would be apt to feel a stronger bias towards their local governments than towards the government of the Union; unless the force of that principle should be destroyed by a much better administration of the latter.[8]

In some prominent instances, Hamilton has been right. The American Civil War and resistance to federally mandated desegregation in the South both suggest the power of citizen attachment to a state. City-by-city resistance to civil rights legislation and school desegregation suggest a power of attachment to the local that resists, in many cases, state pressure. However, current state governments are barely a shadow of what they were two hundred years ago relative to the federal government in power and authority. Under the justification of protecting individual rights, the federal government has gained tremendous influence in all aspects of local government, including education, which in 1787 was not only implicitly excluded from federal purview and explicitly placed under the domain of the state, but was also generally conceived to be an even more local concern than state.

Hamilton ends his argument with the disclaimer that the principle of attachment could be "destroyed by a much better administration of the latter." There is an implicit acknowledgement in this statement that the federal government, metaphorically representing the form of liberalism that privileges individual autonomy, is established in an oppositional vein to state government. Attachment cements the individual to the local unit, but that attachment might be broken through superior performance by the larger unit. Historically, the federal government appears largely to have achieved success in replacing attachment to the state with attachment to the national government, with some notable exceptions. However, the force of the principle of attachment to the local was destroyed less by a "better administration" by the federal government than by an actively interventionist stance practiced by the federal government backed by massive police power. The interventionist stance has been justified by claims of compelling interest in protecting the individual from the actions of states and other local governmental bodies. The federal enforcement of civil rights statutes creates a certain bond between the individual and the federal government.

The larger unit, the federal government, increasingly supersedes the power and undermines the authority of more local units of governance and social organization. Although the power and authority of the state is diminished relative to the federal unit, the state likewise diminishes the power and authority of more local units. However, a delicate balance may exist between the individual's need for local attachment and the power of the larger unit to destroy the force of the principle of inverse attachment. The question remains whether the larger unit can fulfill all the functions of the local.

Let me recapitulate and emphasize: (1) loyalty is an important element in moral conscientiousness in action; (2) loyalty and alienation are oppositionally related; and (3) loyalty to local attachments can be broken down by external and more centralized forces and successes. I believe that a person comes to see herself as a particular being through attachment to ways of being in the world that are cultivated through formal and informal educational conditions.

If one is loyal to one's family, then one is likely to value at least some of those things that members of the family value. If the family values honesty, then one strives to be an honest person, to embody that value and make it not only "mine," but me. The individual gains identity and integrity through developing loyalty to particular manifestations of culture, religion, and/or tradition. Attachment provides the guide for and check on action. The traditions and beliefs an individual attaches herself to, and the particular individuals that manifest those beliefs, provide the source, maintenance, and educative frame of value for the individual member. The truly alienated have no attachments. To be a good person in a good society is to be loyal to that society and to be attached to what it values.[9]

But, the farther removed the focus of attachment, the weaker and more general the attachment is. This only becomes problematic when the more distant (which I refer to as the center, because of its attribute of commonality with reference to the diverse and particular) undercuts the more local. I may seem to have excluded this possibility by emphasizing the strength of the local. However, the center may undermine local attachments without providing an adequately robust replacement. A strictly enforced separation of church and state, for example, may eviscerate a public school's ability to foster commitment in the young to particular social ideals and visions of personal character. If the state is to remain neutral, it cannot coherently replace, in breadth or detail, particular conceptions of the good rooted in a community of practice. If the state were to provide a robust replacement, its claims to neutrality would become less tenable. Charges that public education provides children with instruction in the "religion" of secular humanism arise partly from certain Christian groups who believe that attachment to their values has been undermined, and partly from a fear that the state will replace those values with its own particular and robust sense of the good. This brings us to the crux of the argument.

A fundamental component of political liberalism is its neutral stance toward particular and competing conceptions of the good. However, the liberal state is itself a player in the game. Certain illiberal conceptions of the good cannot be allowed a controlling influence in a liberal state. The liberal state is justified in intervening to prevent holders of one conception of the good from imposing their beliefs on others. The delicate balancing act of the liberal state finds its fulcrum in a minimal set of common beliefs that all included groups can subscribe to. Although more neutral than the robust belief systems it encompasses, political liberalism is not entirely neutral. When supported by the increasingly interventionist power and authority of the center, the impact of that non-neutral component may extend beyond the limits of even relative neutrality and become actively antagonistic toward the foundations of attachment necessary to sustain the identity of constituent groups.

The Hamilton quotation given above may serve as a suggestive metaphor. Liberalism is analogous to the federal government. It seeks to provide a strong but limited center that will hold together disparate groups without unduly oppressing any of them. The operational trademark is the least common denominator. The liberal society professes to respect the autonomy of its component groups, if not of each individual member. This neutral tolerance can exist only if no one conception of the good, other than the minimum which all can agree upon, gains dominance.

A formal system of public education within a liberal framework cannot exhibit partiality. It can provide the source, maintenance, and educative frame only for those minimal ideals that constitute the least common denominator of the beliefs of all the groups that compose the society. In order to maintain its neutral stance, it must be actively antagonistic, through exclusion, to the component ideals that differentiate and make particular any community of belief.

Some have argued that the exclusiveness of this neutral stance has a negative impact on the development of children's character insofar as it separates them from attachment to communities of belief and practice.[10] Others have argued that there is no such thing as a neutral stance in education. Education of the young always involves deep matters of belief and invokes particular conceptions of the good. In this case, the professed liberal neutrality of the state disguises a particular concentration of the good, which is inculcated in youth through the power and resources of the state.[11]

In response to the fears of detachment or replacement mentioned above, some have argued that public education is only one component of the education of our young, and within a liberal society should legitimately refuse the burden of ensuring the holistic development of children. Formal education has only the limited role of transmitting technical knowledge and those virtues necessary for liberal-democratic citizenship. Moreover, the limited scope of public education poses no threat to local communities.[12]

I contend, however, that, similar to Alexander Hamilton and his claims concerning the relative power between the states and the federal government, the center will prove antagonistic to the local. The center does pose a threat to particular conceptions of the good. This threat goes beyond ensuring necessary conditions for the maintenance of a liberal state. The usurpation of the local by the center might not be an educational problem if the center provided a robust conception of the good which would serve as the point of attachment necessary to develop a morally good character. By "robust" I refer to an environmental collection of models and reinforcers that prescribe, proscribe, and problematize patterns of behavior, particular actions, and attitudes with a sufficient richness to provide the myriad experiences necessary for the development of moral perception, judgment, and the integrated self. A particular conception of the good is assumed.

But there are two objections. First, by definition the liberal state cannot provide such a robust conception of the good. Second, liberal conceptions of justice require the liberal state to relate to each individual and community as essentially undifferentiated from all others.[13] Insofar as we attach ourselves to the liberal frame, we detach ourselves from all particulars inconsistent with that frame. Detached from those particulars, we may become alienated from the community that supports them. Unless we replace old attachments with new ones, we risk a personal state of anomie. The liberal frame is characterized by its minimal nature. Insofar as we can attach to it, we are attaching ourselves to a vague collectivity.

Alienation is the status of the sociopath. Attachment to a vague collectivity is an insufficiently robust context for developing the moral self. In a liberal state, the ideological traditions, myths, and rhetorical symbols are not strong enough to support a coherent collectivity over time. Without a coherent collectivity, the individual will be in a circumstance conducive to anomie. If one's circumstances outside the school provide a strong source of particular attachment that is also minimally threatened by the antagonistically neutral context of the school, then one might better resist alienation or anomie. We might describe the same circumstance as one in which particular attachments are broadly consistent with the general attachments of the liberal frame. However, if the intervention of the center extensively detaches succeeding generations of individuals from locally particular attachments, then the basis of support for the local communities disappears.

The relationship of attachment between local communities and the schools serving their youth is pedagogically crucial. In the 1982 book, *High School Achievement: Public, Catholic, and Private Schools Compared*, James S. Coleman, Thomas Hoffer, and Sally Kilgore conclude that student behavior has the greatest single impact on student achievement. They further suggest that student and parent attachment to the school is crucial to good student behavior. In his 1981 *Phi Delta Kappan* article, "Quality and Equality in American Education: Public and Catholic Schools," Coleman puts the case more strongly.[14] Discipline in schools breaks down largely because of a lack of consensus about "the kind and amount of authority over their children [parents wish] to delegate to the school." The lack of consensus creates "a crisis of authority." Consensus is necessary in order to have effective strong academic demands and discipline. In turn, "stronger academic demands and disciplinary standards produce better achievement." Coleman concludes that we should encourage "a pluralistic conception of education, based on 'communities' defined by interests, values, and educational preferences rather than residence." In effect, he advocates creating a system of schools that are particular to the loyalties and attachments of parents and students, including their religious preferences.

In later writings, Coleman further documents the effect of robust agreement or lack of agreement among various components of a child's world. For instance, in one article, he interprets the rise of teen suicide using Durkheim's theory of suicide "as an indicator of the growth in their social isolation."[15] He goes on to argue that schools can provide opportunities, demands, and rewards, but that an intimate environment is necessary for the full development of characteristic attitudes, effort, and a conception of the self. When the relations in the school are formal and legalistic, and families are unable to make up for what the schools do not provide, then there is a drain on the social capital necessary to the development of the good person.[16]

Coleman's analysis is not exactly mine, but his research and arguments are suggestive of the concern I have. His primary concern is with the necessary ingredients to ensure the academic success of students. Only in his latest works does he begin to address the question of the relationship between parent and student commitment to the school, the robustness of the environment (he calls it "intimate"), and the development of good people. Although he does advocate some form of parental choice and a move toward making school environments more reflective of particular communities and more "intimate" environments, he still leans toward tinkering with the mechanics of delivering education instead of addressing the school as a necessary extension of a community.

Tinkering with the mechanics of delivery might be consistent with some version of the local control arguments that currently proliferate. Invoking community control might evoke site-based management, Chicago-style decentralized school boards, or some version of parental choice. The former two miss the concept of community I have in mind. I must stress that I do not conceive of community in geographic terms. Community involves a mutuality of relations of people to each other involving networks of shared emotional bonds or commitments to ideas, practices, and concerns. And, as opposed to favoring the privatization of education, I am more interested in revitalizing an older notion of the public which expands public beyond its currently restricted bounds. This notion of society as composed of various publics cooperating within a larger political and social frame is central to my analysis, and is truer to the historical roots of our own tradition of political liberalism than is a focus on fully autonomous, atomistic individuals would be. It is also consistent with Coleman's requirements for an intimate environment.

In *The World We Created at Hamilton High*, Gerald Grant proves sympathetic to Coleman's research and arguments calling for greater consensus in schools. However, Grant wants to get more specific and discern how an effectively robust climate can be formed in a school. He refers to that climate as the ethos of a school. Ethos is "the spirit that actuates not just manners, but moral and intellectual attitudes, practices, and ideals."[17] In a related article, Grant argues that:

> the moral order of the typical public school became increasingly legalistic and bureaucratic in its reliance on written rules within a centralized administrative hierarchy and in its formalism, impersonality, and emphasis on legal due process.[18]

That reliance on the impersonal characteristics of liberal justice came partly as a result of necessary federal intervention into the education of our children because of the gross inequities that were taking place. However, in some sense the baby may have been thrown out with the bath water. The attempt to adjust for past and present inequities through legislation further removes schools from the influence of local particularities, good and bad. As a result, a legalistic atmosphere pervades the schools. The motivating drive to excel at becoming a particular sort of person is dampened by an institutional emphasis on merely minimizing harm.

In *The World We Created at Hamilton High*, Grant concludes that a strong positive ethos is essential to a high level of academic success in schools, and "ethos depends on agreements about the means and ends of the intellectual and moral order of the school."[19] These agreements have to be "elicited from parents, students, and teachers."[20] Grant is ambivalent about just what is needed in order to establish conditions conducive to the development of that ethos. Generally, though, he agrees to a Coleman-like endorsement for parental choice in schooling, while asserting that morality is independent of religion, and religion is neither a necessary nor sufficient justification for most basic, universal, ethical principles. Implicitly, he suggests that the moral requirements of a liberal democracy can provide a sufficiently robust frame for the education of good people. What is required is some adjustment of the delivery mechanisms, in order for education to gain the strong support of its clients.

Both Grant and Coleman want to keep public schools squarely within the domain of a general public and not release them to the control of assorted publics. The fear of factionalism and provincialism lurking in these arguments, particularly Grant's, is legitimate. The attraction of liberalism, after all, is its promise of protection from the arbitrary use of power and its impartial support of the rights of individuals. To release control of schools completely to local publics is to risk vicious forms of segregation and indoctrination. Prejudice (meant in its most general sense) is a constitutive characteristic of groups with particularized attachments and loyalties. To value something is to give it place in a system of preferences. Unless schools rely on attachment to the liberal society to provide direction, they will have no basis on which to mitigate or thwart destructive, if not evil, localized prejudices. The liberality of society is threatened by the cultivation of too particularistic a set of attachments.

We seem to have arrived at a dilemma. Coleman *et al.*'s and Grant's research suggests the pedagogical necessity of strong loyalty by parents and students to their schools. The schools must reflect or gain the attachments of the parents and children if they are to be effective institutions of learning. From the same research, we learn that schools, to be effective, must engage the entire child, not just some part of her we call citizen or student. The work of Andrew Oldenquist, noted above, suggests that the attachment and engagement must be firm, robust, and particular. We also have reason to fear that local attachments may prove dangerous to, and may even undermine, attachments to the center, and that this is undesirable.

I agree with the need for a robust attachment and the fear that the center may be undermined by too particularized an attachment. I disagree that the center, the least common denominator of the liberal-democratic state, can provide a sufficiently robust environment. And, even if it could, I am unsure that it could, under central administration, achieve the necessary particularity to serve universally as a basis for the loyalty of which Oldenquist writes. Most significant, however, is the tendency to underestimate the centralizing power of the center, as Hamilton seemed to have underestimated the power of the federal government. In trying to balance the need for particularity and local control with the need for impartial, liberal neutrality we must consider the practical effect of that centralized power.

Now let us consider the practical import of recognizing this tension between providing appropriate conditions for the development of a good person and the need for attachment to the center. A primary function of American education, if *Goals 2000* and its predecessor *America 2000* serve as indicators, is to transmit to our children the technical skills necessary to be competitive in a technology-based global economy. Another function, from the same sources, is to ensure that every American has the necessary skills to "exercise the rights and responsibilities of citizenship."[21] Technical and citizenship skills are not sufficient, however. We must also "cultivate values and good character, give real meaning to right and wrong."[22] The functions of American schooling might be reduced to the development of skilled and competitive labor, competent citizens, and members of society having good moral character, at least according to the bipartisan statements of the National Education Goals which have directed Federal education policy since 1991.

In a liberal, pluralistic society, the state has an interest in ensuring the development of good citizens, but it cannot privilege any particular conception of the good which is necessary to the development of a self-integrated, good person. Thus, the National Education Goals have implicit within them a tension between the center and the particular, between competent citizens and individuals of good moral character. They attempt to resolve that tension by advocating parental choice and increased parental involvement in schooling. Still, by emphasizing increased federal involvement in education and the nationalization of curriculum standards and testing, *Goals 2000* fails to recognize or account for the impact of the center on the local. When *America 2000* claims it is "time to turn things around . . . to set standards for our schools— and let teachers and principals figure out how best to meet them," (p. 4) it is either ingenuously promoting a particular conception of the good or failing to recognize the impact of centralized standards on the local. So, too, is *Goals 2000*, when it continues the emphasis on "setting world-class standards that set targets for: what all students should know and be able to do (content standards); and the level of performance we expect students to reach (performance standards)."[23]

Of course, the standards referred to might be minimum in scope and consistent with liberal ideals. In which case, the National Education Goals might be seen as proposing a minimally interventionist liberal umbrella serving to maximize local control of education while ensuring the center's interest in developing good citizens. However, this is not the case. *Goals 2000* is clear on this point. "Rather than just comparing students against each other or setting a minimum criterion for student performance, the National Education Goals call for performance against world-class standards."[24] Saying *what* must be learned, with any degree of specificity, including how such learning is to be measured, becomes tantamount to specifying *how* it must be learned. If "what" and "how" are controlled by the center, what is left for control by the local?

The specific application of the National Education Goals' rhetoric illustrates part of the problem. On March 31, 1992, the Pennsylvania Senate Education Committee voted in favor of revised curriculum and graduation requirements for that state's public schools, to include proven proficiency in learning outcomes. "The outcomes focus on five goals: self-worth, information and thinking skills, learning independently and collaboratively, adaptability to change, and ethical judgment."[25] This appeared to be an attempt to educate the whole child. As might be expected, it did not go unchallenged. The Pennsylvania Coalition for Academic Excellence, a citizens' group with ties to national Christian organizations attacked the goals as " 'value-orientated, attitudinal-based, [and] subjective.' "[26]

As we recognize and try to address the particular and robust nature of attachment necessary for schools to both succeed academically and aid in developing good people, we must carefully work out the relationship between the center and the local. The compromise of teaching "just academics" results in either a stripped-down and anemic education incapable of securing loyalty or a potentially alienating and educationally ineffective environment where there is lack of consensus between the clients and the schools.

Many states are working on ways to accommodate greater local control. Some version of Total Quality Management seems to be attractive as a way to retain central control while taking advantage of the benefits of more localized ideas, needs, and demands. In the early 1990s, New York began to put in place *A New Compact for Learning,* modelled on Total Quality Management ideas. The heart of the compact might be captured by the following statement: The state will define more precisely *what* is to be learned and local districts will decide *how* such learning is to occur.[27]

Without examining specific practices, laws, and policies, it is hard to know exactly what is encompassed by the "what is learned" which the State retains control over and how much control the local has by influencing the "how" of education. I would guess that local influence would actually be pretty minimal under such a plan. The constraints of the center and the liberal nature of the educational institution may allow for somewhat flexible pedagogical methods but would be too constraining to allow for the realization of more robust concepts of consensus in determining the school's ethos. "What is learned," after all, is the very heart of a moral education. And as long as the school community is defined geographically and without effective alternative, then any local consensus must be a compromise of the sort that raises the ire of groups like the Pennsylvania Coalition for Academic Excellence.

Conclusion

Coleman *et al.*'s and Grant's research on effective learning concludes that academic excellence requires congruence between the ethos of the parents and children and the ethos of the school. Oldenquist argues for the particularity of loyalty necessary to prevent alienation and cultivate effective moral conscience. I have argued that the good person must develop within a robust environment supportive of the integrated self. Attachment to liberal virtues is insufficient to secure that robust environment. There is also an explicit contradiction between the need for attachment to particularized conceptions of the good in order to develop a good person and liberalism's commitment to both neutrality among competing conceptions of the good and intervention that effectively excludes and precludes the development of particularized attachment.

The liberal state cannot be the source of a robust educational environment. As long as the center controls the "what is to be learned" of education we must question the ability of schools to operate within those guidelines so as to establish an effective academic and moral learning environment. The control of the state and the tension between the particular and the neutral is further complicated when there is a geographically determined educational community.

There are normative and policy directions strongly implied by my argument. I have presented it in as concrete a fashion as possible because I want this argument to take place in a context in which members of this liberal democracy contemplate and act on school reform agendas. My purpose, however, is not to argue for any particular reform but only to examine what must be taken into account in any effort to educate good people in any good society. As stated above, the nub of the argument is that good people develop within the context of communities which themselves have robust and particular conceptions of what it means to be a good person. Whatever balances we strike in providing the best education we can for the people of this or any society, we must recognize that good people must be valuable members of particular publics before they can be valuable members of a broader society. In a culturally homogeneous state, the education needed to develop valuable members may differ from that needed in a pluralistic society. However, whether the aggregate political unit is homogeneous or pluralistic, attention must be paid to the need for locally particular and robust communities in which children may live and learn.

NOTES

1. "Integrity" is used here in the sense of a self-integrated person, that is, one who is or tries to be coherent in his/her self-identifying actions and intentions. The connotation is of a consistency directed toward realizing a chosen ideal vision of the self. Although honesty, dependability, and steadfastness might be components of this integrated self, they are not definitional. See, Lynn McFall, "Integrity," *Ethics* 98 (October 1987): 5–20.

2. Aristotle, *The Politics of Aristotle*, Ernest Barker, ed., (Oxford: Oxford University Press, 1946), p.102.

3. Community, in this context, does not represent strictly geographic proximity or wide-flung profession-like associations of practitioners or collections of large groups of people. I have in mind something closer to Thomas Bender's idea of a "network of social relations marked by mutuality and emotional bonds." (Thomas Bender, *Community and Social Change*

in America, [New Brunswick: Rutgers University Press, 1978], p. 7.) There must be an experiential component too, so, even more loosely, "community is where community happens." (Bender, p. 6.) Thus, a church congregation, a neighborhood, a group of co-workers, or a group of like-minded individuals who associate with one another might all be considered "community." A community of nations, the medical community, and the human community are ruled out. Community as a political administrative unit, such as a town or current school district, might qualify, but not necessarily, and probably not usually.

4. Andrew Oldenquist, "Loyalties," *Journal of Philosophy* 79, no. 4 (April 1982): 173.

5. *Ibid.*, p. 175. Emphasis in original.

6. *Ibid.*, p. 178.

7. *Ibid.*, p. 182.

8. "Publius," Federalist Number 17, in *The Federalist Papers*, Clinton Rossiter, ed., (New York: Mentor Books, New American Library, Penguin, Inc., 1961), p. 119.

9. Such attachment should not be confused with dogmatic compliance. There is room for a variety of critical positions. Perhaps the most forceful form of critique, the charge that accepted ideals are being trampled upon, is a sure sign of attachment.

10. See, Richard John Neuhaus, "A New Order of Religious Freedom," *First Things* 20, (February 1992): 13–17.

11. Charges that the schools are not neutral have been most recently, and forcefully, brought to light in instances of litigation over the allegedly secular humanist nature of public education. See, *Mozert v. Hawkins County Board of Education,* 827 F2d 1058 (6th Cir. 1987); and Edward F. Sherman, "The Role of Religion in School Curriculum and Textbooks," *Academe* 74, no. 1 (January–February 1988): 17–22.

12. Kenneth Strike, *Educational Policy and the Just Society* (Urbana: University of Illinois Press, 1982), provides an example of those arguments that claim a limited role for non-neutral public education. Amy Gutman, *Democratic Education* (Princeton: Princeton University Press, 1987), provides an example of those arguments that claim no corrosive conflict between public education propagating the civic virtues of the otherwise neutral state and more particularistic conceptions of the good.

13. See Amy Gutmann, "Communitarian Critics of Liberalism," *Philosophy and Public Affairs* 14 (Summer 1985): 313.

14. *Phi Delta Kappan* 63, no. 3 (November 1981): 159–64.

15. James S. Coleman, "Family and Schools," *Educational Researcher* 16, no. 6 (August–September 1987): 32–38.

16. See, James S. Coleman and Thomas Hoffer, *Public and Private High Schools: The Impact of Communities* (New York: Basic Books Inc., 1987); and James S. Coleman, "Schools and the Communities They Serve," *Phi Delta Kappan* 66, no. 8 (April 1985): 527–32.

17. Gerald P. Grant, *The World We Created at Hamilton High* (Cambridge: Harvard University Press, 1988), p.172.

18. Gerald Grant, "Bringing the Moral Back In," *NEA Today* 7, no. 6 (1989): 57.

19. Grant, *Hamilton High,* p.180.

20. *Ibid.,* p.181.

21. United States Department of Education gopher server, *National Education Goals* (last updated April 26, 1994), Goal 5; and United States Department of Education, *America 2000: An Education Strategy Sourcebook* (Washington, D.C.: United States Department of Education, April 18, 1991), p. 4. *America 2000* lists six goals. *Goals 2000* lists eight goals. Of the eight, four are identical to those in *America 2000,* two have been modified, and two are new.

22. *America 2000,* p.6. *Goals 2000* replaces the overt language of character development found in *America 2000* with references to "personal responsibility" and good physical and mental health.

23. National Education Goals Panel, "Building a Nation of Learners," in *The National Education Goals Report* (Washington, D.C.: United States Department of Education, September 1994).

24. Ibid.

25. *Daily Report Card,* an American Political Network, Inc. publication, April 1, 1992.

26. *Ibid.,* April 5, 1992.

27. See, New York State Education Department, *A New Compact For Learning* (Albany: New York State Education Department, March, 1991.)

Jerilyn Fay Kelle

Chapter 4

To Illuminate or Indoctrinate: Education for Participatory Democracy

Introduction

Today, fewer United States citizens participate in their process of self-government than in the past. A recent report by the Harwood Group, indicative of citizens' increasing detachment from public life, reveals that "public participation in voting is low, and seems to be reaching lower levels at each election."[1] In a similar vein, Michael Walzer claims that,

> Increasingly, associational life in the 'advanced' capitalist and social democratic countries seems at risk. Publicists and preachers warn us of a steady attenuation of everyday cooperation and civic friendship. . . . Familial solidarity, mutual assistance, political likemindedness—all these are less certain and less substantial than they once were.[2]

What makes this momentous is that the success of a democracy centers around the involvement of its citizens. Indeed, the Harwood Group concludes that "the health of politics in America is at risk— that perhaps it is even in rapid decline."[3] What makes this controversial are the often radically opposed, competing theories regarding how to frame and to solve this problem.

One theory dismisses the problem at the outset. Its supporters argue that liberalism, the Federalist Constitution, and a capitalist economic order, which are firmly entrenched today—for example, a civil and political economy firmly established with centralization and hierarchy as their chief organizing principles, and undergirded by the values of individualism and the profit motive— were never the appropriate foundations for a participatory democracy requiring an involved citizenry, or workforce. I argue, however, that, ideally, the people of this democracy can renegotiate the terms of their sovereignty as they see fit, difficult as that might be given the present circumstances. Therefore, it is within the purview of the people to re-work that which constitutes the public and their government or political process. If this argument is sound and the Harwood Group's report is accurate, it is of grave concern that there is not a critical mass of citizens willing and able to participate in this debate. Put another way, the critique against liberalism does not negate the fact that a more dynamic political process based on the principles of self-government, liberty from tyranny, and justice, needs a citizenry capable of critical reflection, public discourse, and political activism. And the argument challenging

61

liberalism does not deny the rights of democratic citizens to call for reform, and to propose a participatory democracy.

Let me explain what I mean by "participatory democracy."[4] George Wood distinguishes between "protective" and "participatory" democracies, which he describes as "two polar opposites." He depicts a "protective" democracy as one in which the system's stability is maintained by the actions of an elite minority and the "nonparticipation of the apathetic ordinary man [and woman]."[5] The salient goal in a protective democracy is the protection of a stable political environment. In contrast, a participatory democracy "is conceived as encompassing the broadest participation of the people working to develop political efficacy and a sense of belonging in order to further extend and enhance participation."[6] Wood points out that participants must be decision makers, that they must have access to all the information they need in order to make informed decisions, and "that full participation requires equal power on the part of participants to determine the outcomes of decisions."[7]

In this chapter, I struggle to develop a theory and practice for education in support of a participatory and sustainable democracy. My principal question concerns how a participatory democratic society can prepare its citizens, from kindergarten through graduate school, for democratic, participatory citizenship. I accept this challenge not as an effort to impose an immutable and unitary reality, but as an arguable stand against what I see today as anti-democratic educational practices, such as authoritarian pedagogy, and elitist and objectified (positivistic) epistemology and methodology embedded in education on all levels.

My goal is to join in the discussion about how to envision and implement an education to continue the democratic struggle that began so many centuries ago. The earliest principles of that struggle for American democracy sought to "modify the horizons" of human existence which had been governed by authoritarian elites, dictators, monarchs and despots. Most of us are aware that the world still abounds with authoritarian notions of leadership, education, and government. Yet, it is difficult for most United States citizens to make the same observation about their own country, although others argue that case passionately. This effort, therefore, embodies the belief that education should encourage all participants to be reflective, participatory citizens and develop the critical imagination to interrogate themselves and their wider society as they appear to be, *and* to envision them other than they are.[8] The question is, how can this be done? Some say the answer is called critical pedagogy, or liberatory or transformative education. After researching the possibilities, I concur that critical pedagogy is an excellent beginning.

Arguments for Reforming Educational Practice

Within the rationale of critical pedagogy is a justification, resting upon two arguments, for reforming educational practice and proposing its own, a transformative education, for a participatory democracy. The first argument concerns the nature of learning, and the second what is claimed to be the detriment or liabilities of a "pedagogy of imposition." Before I elaborate on the case that has been made for critical pedagogy, let me elaborate on these arguments.

The first argument is that learning is a lesson to be lived, not talked about; it is to be experienced, as well as reflected upon or intellectualized. Many attribute the essence of this theory to John Dewey. In contrast to Dewey's precepts, which underpinned the early-twentieth-century Progressive movement in education, the predominant practice of educating today is lecturing or teacher-telling, or what Deborah Britzman calls the pedagogy of "imposition."

It is difficult to argue that lecture or teacher-talk is effective in transferring knowledge of the kind that profoundly informs, and that inspires democratic attitudes and actions. Yet current practice remains faithful to "imposition" as its primary medium, which creates experiences that reinforce authoritarianism and elitism, embody the antithesis of democratic attitudes and behaviors, and encourage citizen deference to unchallenged "superiors." We may pontificate in social studies classrooms about the United States of America's being a democratic society. We may even moralize about democratic virtues and behaviors. But if we don't afford students the opportunity within their schools to live in and be active members of a democratic community, they will not become active, participatory citizens in the wider society.

The second argument relates to the first (against a "pedagogy of imposition") and alludes to reasons for opposing direct, moral education. Usually, proponents of moral education propose to solve our problem of lack of democratic virtue and participation by indoctrinating certain values, morals, and qualities that will hopefully engender the kind of moral character needed to enliven a democratic citizenship. The position against this can be explained by reflecting on an article in which Elie Wiesel ponders the resurgence of fanaticism around the globe, including the United States.[9]

Wiesel describes fanaticism as that which "minimizes or excludes all the ideas that confront or oppose it." He tells us that the fanatic shuns debate, and abhors dialog. "He is afraid of pluralism and diversity... he knows how to speak in monologues only. . . . A fanatic has answers, not questions; certainties, not hesitations." What Wiesel claims is at stake in repelling and disarming fanaticism and the hatreds it fuels is no less than "our cultural, ethical and moral future."[10]

I agree with Wiesel, but I find his solution ambiguous. He warns that the way to combat fanaticism is not to "battle it with another kind of fanaticism,"[11] but he doesn't elaborate on what he thinks would constitute that kind of reactionary fanaticism. That is what I address here. I believe a misreading of the causes of both fanaticism and the disintegration of the infrastructures of our democratic society (family, community, and public life) may lead some to infer that the solution lies in enforcing certain codes of moral, ethical, and social behavior.

Although its intent may appear benevolent, that enforcement of "traditional" morals and virtues could be considered yet another form of fanaticism because it comes prepackaged with ready-to-deliver answers, in content and in form. Also, its delivery is usually that of lecture or imposition, wherein an appointed authoritative person—a teacher, an academic or theorist, a political or religious leader, for example—or a standardized curriculum impose a particular code of ethics or behavior on passive recipients. Even though these values and virtues on the surface are favorable to democracy, the "imposition" of them is, by Wiesel's characterization, fanatical, authoritarian, and elitist. Its proponents, claims, and modes of delivery are distanced from ordinary people and ordinary discourse and most often are made difficult or impossible to challenge.

We have tried and have failed to impose codes of ethics and moral behavior in schools and other organizations. The reason for failure may be as Theodore R. Sizer put it succinctly: "A decent person has dignity; to order a person to be decent violates dignity."[12] He also reminds us that, "the expression of decency and efforts to persuade younger folk to adopt the school's values involve judgment and are not matters that can be turned into readily disseminated 'rules.' "[13]

From another angle, consider James S. Coleman's point that corporations have become the principal foundation of our capitalist political economy. They cannot be "socialized" to behave morally; they cannot internalize their behavior in the same way that citizens internalize theirs.[14] Nevertheless, because, in many cases, collectivities are more influential than individuals, we should expect those who run them to ensure that corporations behave ethically. Until that happens, it seems unjust that individuals be held accountable for the moral and ethical well-being of our social, economic, and political culture while corporations are not.

A pedagogy of "imposition," even when indoctrinating individual citizens with "decent" values, still could not help American educational institutions "provide the essential context of responsible citizenship and government."[15] To remain faithful to the principles and practices of self-government and to the advancement of citizens' ability to realize them, attitudes and skills related to participatory citizenship must be expressly taught, in content (the curriculum) and process (the pedagogy or practice), on every level of democratic education. But imposing or indoctrinating certain so-called democratic values or moral virtues in isolation from the political economy and society often begs the issue of providing a context for responsible citizenship or diverts attention away from addressing it.

Transformative Education for a Participatory Democracy

In providing an alternative to imposition, critical pedagogy, or transformative or liberatory education, prepares people not only to survive in current reality but to use their imagination, skills, and experience to transform society into a participatory, sustainable democracy. In other words, critical pedagogy strives to become a transformative educational practice for participants who will learn not only to consume and succeed in today's society, but also to transform it with the express purpose of generating a society with characteristics more participatory, egalitarian, and peaceful—some would even say more moral or decent—than exist today.[16]

Theodore Sizer is a good example among those theorists critical of the *status quo* who proclaim that a vital role of education should be as a public-forming body.[17] He delimits what he calls the "essential claims in education" as being: "literacy, numeracy, and civic understanding."[18] He asserts: "Any community that expects collective, affirmative government requires a literate citizenry," and maintains that "civic understanding" requires "a grasp of the basis for consensual democratic government, a respect for its processes, and acceptance of the restraints and obligations incumbent on a citizen." And, most importantly, he concludes that, "since democracy could not long survive without them, it is reasonable . . . to ensure that each citizen has the means to gain their mastery."[19]

At this point, conservatives usually attempt to discredit liberal or radical educators by labelling them as "politically correct" for professing the need for multicultural, critical, liberatory, and transformational educational practices. As Britzman's insights reveal, conservatives usually ignore the fact that classrooms and schools have always reflected a political, ideological context, usually stoutly conservative. Because we educators participate in the current anti-democratic educational structure, we implicate ourselves as conservative unless we directly place ourselves in an ideological context that questions the status quo.[20]

On the other hand, we may defend our not confronting the political implications of our stance in the classroom by saying that we are limiting our theories and practices to a neutral theoretical enterprise. If we do so, we are only denying its profoundly political and social consequences. Britzman and others assert that neither the structure of teaching, "the normative discourse," nor "what it means to know and learn" are "innocent of ideology."[21] Teaching, Britzman claims, is a political enterprise: "the context of teaching is political, it is an ideological context that privileges the interests, values, and practices necessary to maintain the status quo."[22]

In contrast to the conservatives who claim that teachers can and should maintain neutrality, critical, radical, and feminist educators such as Britzman claim that how we imagine, discuss, and practice education implies core principles which define and authorize political realities. A goal of transformative schooling, then, is to have educators and students alike illuminate education (as well as society in all its complexity) as placed in an ideological context and "unpack" its process and content in critical, and constructive, ways.[23] Transformative education could explicitly serve, also, as a metaphor for life within which there is continual struggle and negotiation over issues of knowledge, truth, and information on the one hand and democracy, freedom, and power on the other.

As a case in point, let's scrutinize the idea that education is distanced from real life, as is implied in the popular maxim that higher education is an ivory tower set above mundane existence. In one way, academics may be uninvolved in community affairs, but education, Ivy League or otherwise, is a vivid, experiential lesson in how we construct and behave in everyday life. For example, the underlying elitism of most universities, their exclusive nature, and limited access and rewards, is replicated in everyday social, economic, and political life: students and community members alike learn very well indeed the lesson that society should be established, appraised, and governed by elites and distant authorities! Academics and students often become distanced from involvement in community affairs and problems, yet these intellectuals set themselves up as the experts to whom communities should turn for advice and policy to solve their problems. This distancing has thwarted the education for a participatory democracy, and illustrates precisely Deborah Britzman's point: education often provides the ideological and political context that privileges some and disempowers others.

Focusing on classroom life, Britzman elaborates, "Power struggles constitute the underlying dynamics of [it], and as such inscribe the content and context of . . . education."[24] She continues with an explication of what is inscribed upon our so-called democratic education by the tensions caused by these power struggles as they are repeated, but seldom openly talked about, across our country today: "Sustaining these tensions are the institutional values of compliance to authority, social conformity, efficiency, standardization, competition, and the objectification of knowledge. Given the authoritarian nature of these values, their realizations require imposition."[25]

Considering education as a practice with serious political consequences, let's examine the "pedagogy of imposition," as opposed to illumination.[26] It can be argued that the "pedagogy of imposition" is the most commonly practiced, and taken for granted, method

of teaching in this country, yet it is counterproductive to the socialization process needed to engender democratic attitudes and behavior. The following illustrates how such a theoretical argument
against imposition would develop concerning the dynamics of classroom life.

R. S. Peters distinguished between *indoctrinating* and *instruct-
ing* by asserting that indoctrination prevents the development of
autonomous critical thought while instruction facilitates its growth.[27]
Educators who indoctrinate become even more anti-democratic and
authoritarian by making any challenge to the knowledge they teach
difficult if not impossible. When educators indoctrinate rather than
instruct their students, they then prevent students from developing their ability to think independently, critically, and creatively.

Deborah Britzman helps me to think about related phenomena from another perspective. Britzman distinguishes between
teacher-student discourses as either authoritative or internally
persuasive. Teacher-student interaction today, she claims, is dominated by "authoritative discourse," characterized as follows: con-
tent-centered and teacher-centered, pre-packaged, acontextual,
lacking "meaningful relationships among the curriculum, the students," and the teacher, privatizing learning, and engendering "exclusions, silences, and resistances."[28] Acting much like imposition
and indoctrination, authoritative discourse seriously limits students'
will and ability to "extend their own knowledge in the process of
coming to know" and become critical and active participants in the
classroom or in the world around them.[29]

In contrast, Britzman presents the reader with a teacher who
encouraged an internally persuasive discourse in her students and
"gave priority to the process of helping students learn."[30] Describing this teacher, Britzman tells us that for her, "content was only
the raw material of the teacher's work; organizing it in meaningful
ways, attending to the diversity of student interests, drawing upon
the creative capacity of students, and orchestrating a pedagogy
that encouraged insight into the material were all a part of the
realization of knowledge."[31] In short, Britzman points out that the
difference between authoritative and internally persuasive discourse
is that the first "attempt[s] to work in spite of students" and the
second "value[s] students as agents in their own learning."[32] It
seems self-evident that if students become agents in their own
learning, they acquire the tools to become active agents in their

own government, in helping to decide their own destiny. It also seems safe to conclude that since indoctrination and authoritative discourse do not allow this sense of efficacy, neither do they allow for the actualization of democratic, participatory citizenship.

Transformative or critical education is designed and implemented with a focus on improving everyone's individual and group life in a participatory and sustainable democratic society. Using a technique called "back-casting" borrowed from environmentalists' discussions about imagining a sustainable future, I will envision what that kind of society and schooling would be like. I'll outline some characteristics of transformative schooling that would advance democratic citizenship. Then, I will talk more about what prevents us from achieving that vision of schooling and democracy.[33]

Vision of a Society
Supporting Transformative Education

Social, political, and economic life would have to provide an environment supportive of transformative schooling. Society, then, would be: a non-elitist and non-authoritarian, participatory or grassroots democracy; politically de-centralized, with community-based economies (a noncorporate-centered political economy); encouraging of social consciousness balanced with recognizing the individuality of its members; more cooperative than competitive; post-patriarchal; non-militarist; non-violent; encouraging of respect for diversity; and concerned with ecological sustainability and global responsibility. As for schools, they would embrace the involvement of the whole community—parents, neighbors, business, churches, political organizations, and local and national social services. School administrators would act as guides, facilitators, and managers sharing power with staff, teachers, students, and community. Faculty members would be empowered and empowering; they would be involved in choices and decisions over structure, schedule, curriculum, discipline, and training. They would be non-elitist and non-authoritarian, student-focused, teachers-and-learners.

The school curriculum would be used to initiate discussion, and not be definitive or limiting; texts would be made purposefully problematic and continually updated. The curriculum as a whole would be relevant, community influenced, and informed, incorporating both the word and the world into the classroom and out into neighborhood and society.[34] Hence, the curriculum would be both theoretical and experiential. It would encourage students to participate in choosing and accenting the material to be used.[35] It would inform contemporary problems with historical interpretation and analysis, and be designed to promote critical thinking, creativity, and problem-solving skills. It would be geared to improving today's conditions and would provide a way to monitor the implementation of our rhetoric, to close the gap between rhetoric and reality. The curriculum would be representative of cultural and ethnic diversity, and would incorporate non-violent conflict resolution skills to deal constructively with differences. It would focus on exposing and eradicating social assaults like sexism, racism, classism, and corporatism; and it would include human and environmental sustainablity in all its goals.[36]

Pedagogy would be authoritative but non-authoritarian, non-elitist and non-impositional, self-conscious and self-reflective, student-focused, dialogic and inclusive, cooperative and participatory, and experiential. It would be not just teacher-telling but teacher-listening; vigilant in making explicit the content, context, and practice of knowledge, power, and authority; diversified; and purposefully problematic and continually updated.

Students would become active in matters of consequence in and outside the classroom, that is, they would be active, problem-solving members in society. They would be learners-and-teachers, creative, and innovative. They would become skilled in critical thinking, consciously independent *and*, at the same time, interdependent, and socially responsible. They would be able to see how their individual situations relate to others', and the wider society.

At this point, I question how much we will have to change in society and schools today to exercise the vision of transformative education. How much will we have to change the way we educate not only students but also teachers? How much will we have to redesign teacher education institutions? At the same time, we who are concerned with the declining vitality of our citizenry and democracy must grapple with particular philosophical and ideological contradictions embedded in our social, economic, and political institutions. These tensions and contradictions have intensified since the industrial revolution, and need to be addressed by political and social theorists concerned with issues of civic education. Examples of these often opaque but powerful contradictions are the following, which are embedded side by side in our social and political consciousness, even in our Constitution:

Individualism vs. Communitarianism

Rights vs. Responsibility

Capitalism vs. Equality

Materialism vs. Spiritualism

Competition vs. Cooperation

Centralization vs. Local Self-rule

Authoritarianism vs. Liberty

Stability and Control vs. Dynamic and Adaptive Citizenry

Conformity vs. Creativity and Innovation

Intellectualism vs. Activism

Patriarchy vs. Freedom

Obedience vs. Vigilance

Only by self-consciously negotiating the tensions between these contradictions, can a modern participatory democracy based on a capitalist economy be made possible and maintained. If citizens and educators are not aware of these contradictions and do not grapple with them in and out of the classroom, as they do not now, the promise of democracy cannot be fulfilled.

As has been argued above, education today, with its pedagogy of imposition and rigidly hierarchical structures, and in its standardized curriculum and evaluation, engenders the antithesis of democratic virtues and behaviors. The cruel irony is that, at the same time, graduates of our schools are blamed for not being active in, and even for rejecting, present-day democratic politics. Citizens who don't get involved in electoral politics or who don't vote are commonly accused of being either apathetic, apolitical, or inept in civic and community life.[37] But seldom noted by their accusers is the fact that until the essentially anti-democratic nature of the United States educational and political system is transformed, our schools and nation will continue to produce neither active participants in our democracy nor economically vital people. If we want responsible and involved citizens, we must come to accept that it is our non-democratic reality that sets the tone for our economic, political, and educational institutions today.[38]

Active democratic citizenship is a focus today in name only. On all levels of education, this gap between rhetoric and reality mocks democracy and becomes a lived tragedy to those who were led to believe in the sovereignty of the people, freedom, and equal opportunity, but have no skills or means to achieve them.

For this reason, I propose that educational theorists work hard to realize another vision of education: A life that is focused on a participatory, democratic citizenship.

Conclusion

In conclusion, I would like to acknowledge the paradox of this proposal. The Harwood Group's report, mentioned earlier in this chapter, which documented serious decline in voter participation, also reported that Americans' faith in our democratic system is deteriorating. "Americans don't believe that 'We, the people' actually rule. They don't believe that the average citizen even influences, much less rules. . . . What is more, people do not believe this system is able to solve the pressing problems they face."[39] The consequences of the lack of faith in the essential nature of the sovereignty of the people are foreboding, as Saul Alinsky's trenchant remarks signify: "From time to time there have been external enemies at our gates; there has always been the enemy within, the hidden and malignant inertia. . . . There can be no darker or more devastating tragedy than the death of man's faith in himself and in his power to direct his future."[40]

The paradox seems inescapable. The only ones who can alter that inertia and regain the power to direct our own future are ourselves. But when most of us are educated in followership, civic indifference, and passivity, rather than in leadership, civic vigilance, and participation, where and how can we ordinary citizens begin to act responsibly and democratically to sustain the public good? Can we reform public space and restore faith in ourselves to direct our future by demanding the kind of education that will enable us to do it? From classrooms to the principal's office, from local school boards to federal conference rooms, could we, students, teachers, citizens, and officials reclaim public schools as critical sites for the struggle over and creation of a democratic participatory society? Intentionally establishing this democratic purpose for public schooling, to prepare ourselves to become participatory, sovereign, and just people, is only one way to begin, but without this one, I argue, other strategies will most likely continue to fail.

NOTES

1. The Harwood Group, "Citizens and Politics, A View from Main Street America," (Dayton: The Kettering Foundation, 1991), p. 1.

2. Michael Walzer, "The Civil Society Argument," Chantal Mouffe, ed., *Dimensions of Radical Democracy, Pluralism, Citizenship, Community* (New York: Verso, 1992), p. 90.

3. The Harwood Group, p. 1.

4. For other arguments calling for radicalizing democracy as we know it, see Chantal Mouffe, ed., *Dimensions of Radical Democracy, Pluralism, Citizenship, Community.*

5. George Wood, in "Schooling in a Democracy: Transformation or Reproduction?", *Educational Theory* 34, no.3 (Summer 1984): 219.

6. *Ibid.*

7. *Ibid.*

8. This is a hallmark of critical theory, but here I'm thinking particularly of its use in Maxine Greene's *The Dialectic of Freedom* (New York: Teachers College Press, 1988), and in Greene, foreword to Deborah Britzman, *Practice Makes Practice,* (Albany: State University of New York Press, 1991).

9. Elie Wiesel, "When Passion is Dangerous," *Washington Post*, Sec: WSP, April 19, 1992: 19–20.

10. *Ibid.*

11. *Ibid.*

12. Theodore R. Sizer, *Horace's Compromise, The Dilemma of the American High School*, (New York: Houghton Mifflin Company, 1992), p. 125.

13. *Ibid.*

14. James S. Coleman, *The Asymmetric Society* (Syracuse: Syracuse University Press, 1982), p. 96.

15. Sizer, *Horace's Compromise*, p. 86.

16. Costa Criticos, University of Natal, Durban, South Africa, helped me to think through this conceptual framework of education as generative rather than simply consumptive.

17. For historical and contemporary accounts embellishing the role of education as a public-forming body, especially for democracy, also see: Pangle and Pangle, *The Learning of Liberty: The Educational Ideas of the American Founders* (Lawrence, Kansas: University Press of Kansas, 1993); Robert B. Westbrook, *John Dewey and American Democracy* (New York: Cornell University Press, 1991); and, Walter Feinberg, *Japan and the Pursuit of a New American Identity, Work and Education in a Multicultural Age* (New York: Routledge, 1993).

18. Sizer, *Horace's Compromise*, p. 86.

19. *Ibid.*

20. Some feminist educational theorists argue this, such as Patti Lather, *Getting Smart, Feminist Research and Pedagogy with/in the Postmodern* (New York: Routledge, 1991); and, Elizabeth Ellsworth, "Why Does Not this Feel Empowering? Working Through the Repressive Myths of Critical Pedagogy," *Harvard Educational Review* 59 (1989): 297–324. For a critique of critical pedagogues who inadvertently impose their own ideological "regime," see Jennifer Gore, *The Struggle for Pedagogies: Critical and Feminist Discourses as Regimes of Truth* (New York: Routledge, 1993).

21. Britzman, *Practice Makes Practice,* p.11.

22. *Ibid.*

23. Often critical theorists address education as a political enterprise. Addressing common classroom situations, see: Ira Shor and Paulo Freire's *A Pedagogy for Liberation, Dialogues on Transforming Education* (Boston, Mass.: Bergin & Garvey Publishers, Inc., 1987); and, *Freire for the Classroom, A Sourcebook for Liberatory Teaching* (Portsmouth, N.H.: Boynton/Cook Publishers, 1987).

24. Deborah P. Britzman, "Who Has the Floor? Curriculum, Teaching, and the English Student Teacher's Struggle for Voice," *Curriculum Inquiry* 19, no.2 (1989): 150.

25. *Ibid.*

26. Britzman, *Practice Makes Practice*, p. 148.

27. R. S. Peters, *Authority, Responsibility and Education*, (London: George Allen and Unwin, 1973).

28. Britzman, *Practice Makes Practice*, p. 114.

29. *Ibid.*, p. 185.

30. *Ibid.*

31. *Ibid.*

32. *Ibid.*

33. This sketch is a composite derived from the synthesis of several critical theories, therefore, any one critical theorist may not subscribe fully to the whole vision as I have conceived and presented it.

34. Paulo Freire often refers to the need for schools to teach how to become literate in not only "the word" but "the world."

35. Britzman (*Practice Makes Practice*, p. 182) talks about curriculum as being "developed in the pedagogical encounter," which I think should be an essential principle of critical and transformative education.

36. About critical pedagogy incorporating a more viable position on environmental concerns, see William F. Pinar and C. A. Bowers, "Politics of Curriculum: Origins, Controversies, and Significance of Critical Perspectives," in *Review of Research in Education*, Gerald Grant, ed. (Washington, D.C.: AERA, 1992).

37. Sheldon Wolin characterizes current anti-democratic conditions in the United States while discussing how citizens act not from apathy but from the desire to reject participation in an anti-democratic system; see his "What Revolutionary Action Means Today," in *Dimensions of Radical Democracy: Pluralism, Citizenship, Community*, Chantal Mouffe, ed. (New York: Verso, 1993), pp. 240–253.

38. Similar conclusions have been drawn by many others, in particular, C. Wright Mills, *The Power Elite* (New York: Oxford University Press, 1956); James S. Coleman, *The Asymmetric Society* (Syracuse: Syracuse University Press, 1982); and, William Greider, *Who Will Tell the People, The Betrayal of American Democracy* (New York: Simon & Schuster, 1992).

39. The Harwood Group, p. 1.

40. Saul Alinsky, *Rules for Radicals*, (New York: Random House, 1971).

Zeus Yiamouyiannis

Chapter 5

Subverting the Capitalist Model for Education: What Does It Mean to Educate Children to be Valuable Members of a Valuable Society?

Introduction

Most discussions around the education, especially the moral education, of children are inappropriately dominated by nostalgia. We all seem to want what's best for children, to give them the best of what we have. We want them to be mature, responsible, valuable members of present society, yet we prepare them for the society we once occupied, not for the one they do and will occupy.

The responsible adult teacher transmits and models values of empathy, responsibility, concern, discipline, and joy as developed through tradition. Children require structure and benefit from the sense of continuity that tradition provides. Both are necessary. Neither is sufficient. If education centers merely on structure and the sense of continuity that tradition provides, the child is left to thrash out an identity alone and to haphazardly develop abilities to understand change and create *new* values coextensive with the old.

The context of society changes over time, bringing different moral demands. This fact is still rarely considered seriously in the practical education of children. Adults often merely transmit the values of hard work, competition, rugged individualism, "playing the game", listening to a dominant voice, inherent to a capitalist, industrial society which is declining. The crucial skills of collaboration, participation, initiation, expression, listening to and understanding many voices and many cultures, inherent to the emerging democratic, post-industrial society, are largely ignored or given token attention.

We may ask: "Why are the moral values needed for functioning in present society ignored by adults in their education of children?" The simple answer is: "Adults themselves have not learned these values and do not know how to enact them." If moral education means that an adult *inducts* a child into values and knowledges that the adult already has acquired and retained, then the adult must by definition ignore those values or knowledges, needed or not, which he or she has not acquired or retained.

With an exclusive emphasis on moral and civic "education as induction," or, in Paulo Freire's terms, the "banking concept" of education,[1] capitalist, industrial society has produced a maladaptive value with regard to the nature and purpose of education itself: Education is something done by one party to another, by adult to child, by ascribed producer of knowledge to ascribed consumer of knowledge. If the adult does not know enough about the emerging society, the children he or she teaches will be ill-prepared to become valuable members of that society. In a post-industrial society, with the emergence of new voices and a tremendous diversification of information, it has become impossible for the adult to possess enough knowledge to prepare children adequately according to this model.

Need for an Alternative Concept of Education

Changing context demands an alternative concept of education, entailing different values, one which relies as heavily upon accessing, exchanging, and integrating knowledge as on possessing and reproducing it. Children and adults must, therefore, both learn to communicate and receive knowledge. Education cannot be something merely done by the adult to the child because this would leave the child unprepared to be the active, valuable participant in the creation, not merely reproduction, of a moral society. The *value* of "education as reciprocation," as well as "education as induction," requires a moral commitment on the part of the adult to model reciprocation in educative settings, by eliciting the knowledge of children, learning from them, and helping them learn from one another. Perhaps this is what it means, then, to educate children to be valuable members of a valuable society today.

Adults may have skills gained through experience, such as the ability to reason and articulate, but these are fruitfully invigorated with a child's knack for open-mindedness, novelty, sympathy, and curiosity, which often becomes eroded in adults. Children do not have to have the immediate, fully developed ability to reason in order to make observations and develop links between those observations and the organization of society.

In many ways the argument about when children are developed enough to reasonably articulate their insights is irrelevant and smacks of an elitist, "club" mentality when it comes to membership into an educative society. When children feel their worth from the start by being encouraged to express their knowledge and listen to the knowledge of others, they are already developing the skills for solid, democratic participation. If he or she is challenged and supported by others and guided by the teacher, an average child will learn more quickly how to reason, because he or she is gaining experience in an interpretive framework that has room for and can be influenced by his or her understanding, and thus the child will be more motivated to understand that interpretive framework.

When children start to reason well enough to articulate their insights more clearly, the benefits of their contributions become even more recognizable. Twenty to thirty active young minds coming up with suggestions and observations provide a much richer atmosphere than one teacher pedantically transmitting ideas from a textbook. In order for class participation to be substantive (that is, influence feelings, knowledge, and possible solutions to a problem) there must be some systematic way in which a child's "imperfect" articulation can be listened to, worked with, and incorporated into the larger body of knowledge in the classroom and possibly beyond.

Let's take a classroom example. Soon after being introduced to the fundamental concepts of global warming, for instance, children might be encouraged to share their experiences and feelings concerning the environment and things that endanger the environment. From this narrative source, the teacher learns what is relevant and important to the students, which provides a ground for discussion of larger issues and development of useful scientific, affective, political, and moral skills.

Instead of just memorizing a small class of "solutions" and making a few lifestyle changes to cut down on the use of certain products which exacerbate the warming problem (the education-as-consumption approach), children might be taught how to measure for the presence of warming gases, research environmental trends related to global warming, and delve perhaps into media presentation or misrepresentation of global warming to see to what degree global warming is a problem. Whether warming is bad might even be discussed along with projected consequences of global warming.

Having gained a context in which to work, and in this case become aware, with the teacher's help, that warming is a problem, children might then be encouraged to identify elements or products that contribute to warming. They might then come up with ways to decrease their use in the local community and/or suggest replacements. This whole process of combining teacher-knowledge with the more specific student-knowledge becomes a good ground from which the children may teach the community (perhaps in the context of a "Keep the Planet Cool" campaign) about global warming and the ways in which the community might do its part to slow it.

Other issues arise as the consequences of this education project bring other questions. What would the decrease in the use of certain products do to the economy? Instead of the teacher's saying, on getting a response to that question from a student, "That's a good idea, Maria," and giving her some "bonus points" for creativity and reasoned thinking, the teacher helps draw out Maria's idea into the social and educational medium of the classroom, where it is conceptually worked out, along with its potential impact, consequences, and latent implications.

If this educational scenario seems to recall Dewey's experiential education, it is not by chance.[2] However, I would not call it wholly Deweyan. In many ways, the implications within the aforementioned scenario extend far beyond pragmatism and its emphasis on informed decision making based on deliberation about lived consequences, into the creation of new sources for sensibilities and sensitivities in education, for the teacher as well as the student.

Dewey's notions were formed within an industrial context and at a time when positivism held a lot more sway upon the forms that inquiry was expected to take. The present context is post-industrial and in many ways post-positivist. The model for inquiry within positivism centers around recognizing a problem, forming hypotheses for a solution, and experimenting with alternative hypotheses and assessing them against some sort of objective standard in order to come up with the best solution.

Students Contribute to Analysis and Solution of Problems

Postindustrial problem-setting requires a more nuanced analysis of why certain people experience something as a problem and others do not. What may be a problem for a middle-class teacher of English ancestry may not be a problem for a working class, Italian-American student like Tony, and vice versa. This only reaffirms the need to include the contributions of students in their own education. Assessment of possible solutions to a problem, under post-positivism, involves an interpretation that can never be wholly objective, as assumed under positivism. In fact, objectivity may increasingly involve opening up assessment to a wider audience than that of experts who tend to share similar ethnic, gender, and class backgrounds.[3] Anti-naturalist advances in philosophy and sociology have led to a recognition of a wider range of influences, such as intersubjectivity, in the personal construction of knowledge and evaluation of consequences.[4]

Seeing everything educational in terms of problems is itself problematic. Discussions and judgments around environmental issues, as well as moral issues, for instance, involve explorable sensibilities, and not just problems to be analyzed. Many of the challenges we face involve aspirations, motivations, personal history, in short, a context, explained better in a narrative than in a lab report.[5] Though a science-like qualitative research can be systematically applied to narrative, it can neither fully capture nor replace the power of narrative. As the importance of context and narrative gains credence within moral inquiry, I expect that the way we conduct inquiry and perceive the world around us will alter fundamentally.

Students May Question Societal Values

The very environment in which learning and teaching takes place influences how and what one learns. In the traditional industrial classroom, Tony and Maria unconsciously learn whose knowledge is valued—the teacher's—through the positioning of grids of desks all facing the teacher. Collaborative classrooms where desks are positioned in clusters or in a circle attest by their physical arrangement to the importance of student input. Regular classes that include disabled students teach children that we are all expected to live and learn together, that we are all valued members. Special classes, on the other hand, be they for learning-disabled or gifted children, inspire a stratified, classified concept of the world.

Let us now concentrate on an internal problem with how education, and particularly moral and civic education, is conducted. Even within the classroom, where the forms of logic and grammar are at least partially grasped by all the participants, say, in a typical American high school, those capable of reason are not "taken seriously." They are encouraged to express that reason only in ways already sanctioned by the teacher.

Because it has been burdened with the industrial model, past American schooling, conservative as well as liberal, seems to have had more to do with trying to get reasoning beings to accept what is already established as correct than to question and contribute to a definition of correctness. The children are expected to accept a basic contradiction: they are supposed to reason in order to accept an unassailable definition, that is, something beyond reason. Rather than have the sense to ask questions that reflect a democracy: "Is this particular democracy working? Does it match the ideals of our society? How might we improve and redefine it?", educators make ironic, autocratic assertions like, "Democracy works. Let's see how any reasonable, moral person would accept democracy."

The right answer is already in the adult teacher's head. What need has school for real critical thinking? In order to conduct a legitimate inquiry and make "good" judgments, it is supposedly necessary for me as a student to submit rationally to this process of moral consumption, without which I am unqualified to participate in society as a member. Yet the membership process produces habits that have a heavy cost. In present education, a student "takes in" maybe two decades' worth of learning before he or she is allowed to teach, by which point critical and creative capabilities have become atrophied and expression neglected. These consumption habits are more likely to produce the docile, untroublesome student and citizen than the vibrantly moral one. It is no wonder to me that bright and moral young people resist or rebel against a system that claims to love them but has no room for their stories or their unconditional critical contribution. All too often, the product of a practice founded upon such a conception of education is a student who resists or rebels against being taken over, or who resigns him- or herself to the limited power of deciding selectively which information will make its way into his or her head.

In traditional education, educating children to be valuable members of society involved a somewhat impositional process not quite as violent as force-feeding (though there have been instances where this analogy is accurate), whereby an adult persuades, through reinforcements like praise and the withholding of punishment, a child to eat (that is, adopt) certain capitalist and liberal democratic attitudes. Discipline was valued and reinforced because it could train the minds and bodies of students to develop traits functional for a capitalist, industrial society—those that allowed

students to chug through given work and given problems stead-
fastly, if unimaginatively. Punctuality, quietness, hard work, and
even submissiveness were examples of appropriate behaviors or
evidence of certain virtues, like patience and self-control, required
for the craft of living in a hierarchically organized capitalist and
industrial world.[6] Such habituation resulted in the development of
a disposition that lent itself to the establishment of a pliable, hard-
working citizen.[7]

The child in this kind of education is reduced in many important respects to a mere audience. Important decisions regarding
the foundations of proper lifestyle are made elsewhere, by others,
by experts, as are the philosophical bases of judgments regarding
moral good and bad.[8] The normal person's virtue lies not in making
but submitting to and deciding how to make manifest certain pre-
established policies. Those who feel entitled and have access to the
appropriate mechanisms, usually by virtue of a social status often
based in race, class, and gender, are the ones who make their way
into presiding expert or leadership positions—positions only reinforced by circular empirical research, which shows such privileged
people to be natural leaders by virtue of their predominance among
leadership ranks.

Equal representation of views is a requirement of democracy.
Yet traditional education does not emphasize the independent articulation and representation of diverse views. Under the guise of
democracy, privileged views promulgated as reasonable by education mechanisms favor the development of a leadership elite, narrow in ideal and in class, race, and gender representation. The
tools of leadership favor the values and education of those already
in power, making it difficult for those who are unentitled even to
access the mechanisms needed to engage fundamental philosophical and political issues. Such access requires practice in being heard
and challenged, a practice rarely seen in much traditional schooling.

Liberal education improves upon the often brute authoritarianism of traditional so-called education, but is still primarily
interested in the reproduction of expected traits at the expense of
time spent discussing their desirability. The only difference between liberal education and traditional education is that the expectations and traits for successful membership in society have
changed. Neither form of education values reasonable but
unsanctioned questioning. Where traditional education was

willing to settle for the reproduction in schools of certain behaviors, liberal education demands the cultivation within children of their "own" attitudes and sentiments, which are then supposed to produce the expected reasonable behavior associated with so-called rational deliberation.

In this way, children's behavior is, supposedly, not imposed, because it has origins within the sentiments of the child. The child has been inculcated with the proper moral "inner life," as Amy Gutmann, among others, has called it.[9] The child is now uncontroversially and uncoercively moral, having been taught certain virtues in such a way that they have become the child's own. Such reasoning is incomplete, however. Liberal education has still failed to include the original and self-conscious constitution of children in the formation of desirable sentiment. Liberal moral education has taken the form of a sleight-of-hand conservatism, reasserting and transmitting those particular morals and civic values that result in expected responsible action among those so educated.

I will grant that a minimum amount of moral vocabulary will be imposed upon children, through mimesis, that is, the habituation into certain ways of thinking and expressing that come as a consequence of the daily life of any human society. Certain values like kindness, generosity, loyalty, and trustworthiness are necessary for the operation of most, if not all, societies. These might be called *intrinsic*, or operational, values. However, there is a difference between the values necessary for any democratic society's operation and those *functional* values necessary for the so-called glory of a capitalist, industrial society or for any dominant vision within democracy. Many concepts like equality, a value necessary for operation, have been linked to a tacit and paradoxical Orwellian " . . . but some are more equal than others" when attached to a capitalist, industrial vision within democracy.

Resisters of such a tacit imperative, do not normally find their resistance through formal education. Instead, formal education has provided a mechanism whereby students learn to accept or even take advantage of the inequalities and contradictions within a struggling democracy. Children from privileged backgrounds are encouraged to develop their intelligence and increase their advantages in special "gifted" programs, rather than to share their knowledge and learn from the knowledge of others. Members of underrepresented groups in higher education often swap tales of having to fight to be heard by people unfamiliar and uncomfortable with their brands of knowledge. An education that does not actively value the awareness and reasoning of all its people in the formation of their own sentiments may be capitalist but is not democratic.

Our education can perhaps claim that it forwards the ideas of proper shame at wrongdoing, but it has been complicit in encouraging such a concept to be used in particular and often in inappropriate and self-oppressive ways. There are many who have been taught to feel shame or even self-hate merely for having black skin. For every person who feels guilt at having cheated on a test, there is another who feels guilty or shamed for being homosexual, for being poor, or for not trying hard enough to satisfy this or that authority.

Both traditional and liberal education assume a capitalist mode of conduct. The adult teachers are producers and suppliers of knowledge distinct from the consumers, who are children. This leaves both teachers and students helpless to question the nastier implications of capitalist operation. It is quite clear, for instance, that children can be taught by commercials to desire Brand X or Toy Z, and to feel pained when they do not get what they desire. A similar schema is being established through commercials, as through liberal education. Though the behavioral and attitudinal goals of commercials may not be as noble, they are still the product, as are much traditional and liberal education, of a little-questioned, though not unreasoned, acceptance and internalization of certain sentiments. As educators, I think we have seriously to entertain the notion that we have been trained to sell children a certain moral disposition by persuading them to want it, albeit not as effectively as advertisers sell G.I. Joes and Barbie dolls. Alas! Gold stars and good grades do not seem to have the same persuasive power as Teenage Mutant Ninja Turtles. But for all the talk about child-centered education, where is the child who is acting, interacting, participating, and producing? What often motivates so-called child-centered educations are nostalgic notions about how children feel, and adult ideas about what the child wants and needs (and, implicitly, what the child ought to be).

Reciprocal Teaching and Learning

At this point, I would like to revisit our original question: "What does it mean to educate children to become valuable members of a valuable society?" In the context of this discussion, it means that all members of a democratic society, adults and children, the economically and politically powerful and the powerless, must commit themselves to creating conditions for a reciprocal teaching and learning among people and peoples within a society. Adults have a special responsibility, because their children are initially so dependant upon them, for providing educative arenas which evoke self-directed, socially responsive participation. In her chapter, my colleague, Fay Kelle, has offered specific political and social ways of doing so. I would like to focus on what I feel to be the philosophical/conceptual issues surrounding this issue.

Perhaps we might first examine what happens when we involve the fresh, untutored minds of children in distinguishing between what I have referred to as operational or "intrinsic" values (like trustworthiness, compassion, and/or a generic willingness to work and commit oneself to a project) and what I have termed "functional" values (the shape intrinsic virtues take when placed within a capitalist context). Functional values often like to masquerade as intrinsic values. Capitalist dogma, for instance, often identifies a good person as one who has a good job. Yet an open-minded discussion in an elementary classroom could powerfully break such an identification and help free children from the mystique of unexamined dogma. It would not be surprising to hear a child say in response to this good person = good job equation, "I knew someone who lost her job and she was a very nice woman." If I were a teacher involved in this discussion, I might use this comment as a springboard into a collective analysis of the advantages and disadvantages in our society and possibly, depending on the extent of the discussants' interests and capabilities, of capitalism in general. We could look for ways to improve the opportunities for people to gain worth by finding other ways people can feel good about themselves than by having a job. This would be important especially to youngsters, who will not work for some time to come.

Let me take this opportunity to answer a criticism of this idea I received from a colleague: "You are imposing your vision of a proper education, just as everyone else is. What sets you apart from everyone you have been criticizing?" By no means am I suggesting that I have no vision or conviction when engaged in instruction with children. Children "become aware" partly through the ideological influence I cannot help but exert when I attempt to aid their own understanding of moral issues. This is a reality. If one wants to call this imposition, then it is of a different kind from the ideological insistence that seeks to extract "correct" moral answers from children.

Some imposition is an intrinsic necessity. Democracy involves the formation of, and participation in, reasonable options, but not wanton license. My imposition merely increases the range and opportunity for different voices to be heard and different knowledges to have effect; it does not sanction license any more than it sanctions mindless privileging of particular knowledges, be they reasoned or not. Both license and privilege hamper democratic potential by overrunning or silencing certain members. As explained earlier, traditional and liberal education are guilty of the latter. My vision may not be perfect, but it is more democratic and allows a wider discussion of democracy.

My vision is flexible, and is open to influence from the opinions of those children who have developed the capacities to teach and relate their own visions. We all have ends-in-view, as Dewey says, and reasons for acting in a particular way; these should be brought to discussions overtly.[10] Without heavy-handed or automatic privileging of one vision, perhaps a composite vision can be worked out which will far outstrip the limited power of a single-minded conception. Hopefully, the example I provide as a teacher within and outside a classroom will serve to further make it clear where I stand.

There is no getting around the fact that an imposed vision of inclusion and mutual participation within a moral discussion will have empirically different educational effects than a producer/consumer conviction. The problem comes in rating the effects. I would insist that the children's own feelings of satisfaction and development of communication and synthesis and conflict resolution skills be part of any assessment of effects. I can moralize as to the characteristics of Nazi Germany that made it an inferior moral society, and give good reasons, but this does not encourage children to develop a skill in inquiring into the nature and foundations of morality itself. There is far more educational power created when the moralities of both our own and other societies are examined and critiqued by the uninitiated, like children. They are inside our society and thus know it in a sympathetic way, yet have not completely bought into its imperatives. Children thus are in a unique position to give an internal critique (as opposed to the external critique given by adults in other cultures) on American society and its hypocrisies, and often do so with uncomfortable regularity. However, instead of being brushed aside, as they normally are, children's critical observations should be taken seriously.

The consumer/producer model of moral education does not provide a good ground for internal critique, because its very set-up springs from adult "moral" assumptions as to the correctness of certain ways of relating knowledge, which are not really open to question or influence.

Conclusion: Requirements for a More Equitable Moral Discussion

I would like to conclude by asking, "What is required for a more equitable moral discussion which might make us active and knowing moral teachers of one another?" I would like to list and explain some recommendations I find primary to such a discussion.

First, make moral language something not merely to be acquired, but grappled with and expanded. In other words, do not merely request that people assimilate into a moral vocabulary constructed primarily by noted philosophers and sociologists, without also working to make that language assimilate to the experiences and reasoning of ordinary people. The purpose of moral education is not to make moral experts but to find better, more humane ways to conduct ourselves and conceive of conducting ourselves around one another. Involved in this is the substantive and recognized inclusion of narratives in moral talk.

Second, do not always confuse idealism with ideology in educative contexts involving moral education. There is a strong tendency to think that a person's moral opinion is an inflexible, unreasonably universalized, and thus discountable, moral recommendation. People's moral opinions should be both challenged and supported, and, perhaps, partly incorporated into the construction of a larger, enriched moral schema. There are very few opinions that should simply be disallowed. Flaws in moral reasoning should not be seen as reasons to throw out moral opinions wholesale. Postmodern skepticism should be used as a positive tool to keep people informed of weaknesses in systems of moral conceptualization, and as evidence for the need for a multi-individual and multi-cultural construction of what constitutes a moral life.

Third, admit of more than rational/hierarchical ways of structuring and assessing moral inquiry. Moral inquiry is not simply a sterile empirical and rationalistic exercise. Though rationalism and empiricism can be useful in moral inquiry, reading a novel can be a form of moral inquiry. This brings up the inclusion of other types of knowledge—such as affective, emotive, and tacit—in the assessment of morality. "How does something make you feel and why?" Break the monopoly of traditional hierarchies of moral reasoning and other forms of so-called objective moral assessment that fairly burst at the seams with moral assumptions regarding the rightness of particular modes of order and organization in viewing human phenomena. Emphasis in moral policymaking should be directed away from the aristocratic control of the less morally sophisticated toward the inclusive construction of moral forums, which might then generate possibilities to be used at broader levels of societal organization.

Adults do have a serious responsibility in the education of children. We hold great physical and mental power over children, and cannot help but exert that power every time we care for children. But children have power also. They have the power to care, to see with uncanny ability everything from beautiful possibilities to our hurt as adults. They have a power to speak their minds and exert their identities. Together, we need to form our world, because practically speaking, amidst growing chaos, we need every available heart and mind. A child needs respect as do we adults. We should be comforted by their aid, and by the realization that we do not need to know everything to provide our children with what they need. We have to help children learn the best of our knowledge and how to create, organize, and add to it the best of their knowledge. The sooner we start, the better. The world that results will be the combination of all our best efforts.

NOTES

1. Paulo Freire refers to "banking education" throughout his book, *Pedagogy of the Oppressed* (20th anniversary edition), translated by Myra Bergman Ramos (New York: Continuum, 1993). He juxtaposes it with a conversational relationship between teacher and student, which he favors.

2. See John Dewey, *Democracy and Education* (New York: Macmillan and Co., 1916), especially chapters 11, 12, and 13: "Experience and Thinking," "Thinking for Education," and "The Nature of Method."

3. Sandra Harding develops this idea in more depth in her book, *Whose Science, Whose Knowledge?* (New York: Cornell University Press, 1991).

4. Fred Dallmayr and T. McCarthy, eds., *Understanding and Social Inquiry* (Notre Dame: University of Notre Dame Press, 1977) details some of these anti-naturalist advances of theorists like Peter Winch, Charles Taylor, and Jurgen Habermas.

5. In *Narrative Knowing and the Human Sciences* (Albany: State University of New York Press, 1988), Donald Polkinghorne discusses the importance of narrative and language in not only denoting but *shaping* language.

6. For a thorough exegesis on the development of traditional industrial education mechanisms as they interacted with the growth of industries and professions, see David Noble, *America By Design: Science, Technology, and the Rise of Corporate Capitalism* (New York: Knopf, 1982).

7. David Tyack and Elisabeth Hansot, *Managers of Virtue: Public School Leadership in America, 1820–1980* (New York: Basic Books, 1982), especially pp. 129–167, brings to light that children are not the only people in education routinely deskilled and stripped of agency. Though teachers have a kind of power in the classroom, they are often treated as "children" by the administrative elite, termed by Tyack and Hansot "the educational trust."

8. The instilling of "proper moral sentiments" in children eerily echoes those mechanisms for self-policing described in Michel Foucault's *Discipline and Punish* (New York: Vintage Books, 1977). See, especially, in Part III, discussions of the production of "docile bodies" and the architecture, the Panopticon, of self-policing.

9. See Amy Gutmann, "Undemocratic Education," in *Liberalism and Moral Life*, Nancy Rosenblum, ed., (Cambridge: Harvard University Press, 1989), pp. 71–88.

10. Dewey, *Democracy and Education*, p. 106

Barbara McEwan

Chapter 6

Assaulting the Last Bastions of Authoritarianism: Democratic Education Meets Classroom Discipline

Introduction

Currently, our public schools are under the bright light of scrutiny, as media attention increasingly focuses on student disciplinary problems. Persons representing a variety of private and public interests vie with each other to determine the means by which students may be taught respect, cooperation, and moral values. A perceived lack of respect and increasing incidents of violence are cited as the impetus behind this concern over how students are disciplined and schools managed. With many perpectives represented, the battle is being joined over whose values will be taught and how values will be imparted. Democratic education, certainly not a new idea, is being discussed as one approach to helping young people learn and practice their civic responsibilities.

It has been my experience, however, that, in many schools, the methods for carrying out democratic practices day-to-day are either not clearly understood or not carefully adhered to. As a result, strategies for implementation vary widely from one setting to another. I have observed that these differing strategies often result in so much contradiction in discipline and curricular techniques that confusion, and even animosity, is aroused among students, parents, and educators.

This chapter will offer an alternative approach to democratic schooling titled Judicious Discipline, a model that provides a consistent and holistic approach to teaching young people the democratic values embedded in the United States Constitution through their daily interactions with teachers and administrators.

While many educators are willing to employ democratic *curriculum* strategies, my observations suggest they are often much less willing to incorporate democratic *management* strategies into their schools and classrooms. Although educators may espouse a belief in democratic schooling, their approach to managing students often reveals another, more autocratic, perspective. I believe that curriculum and management strategies that lack the democratic concepts of equity and tolerance can lead to curious contradictions in classroom practices.

When observing the contradictions in education, I have found the strangest of all to be the perspective of some educators that classroom management strategies based on fear, competition, and intimidation comprise the most effective ways to teach students the democratic value of personal responsibility. Although most new curriculum concepts, from developmentally appropriate practices to authentic assessment, aim at creating more equitable learning environments, these innovations have not yet been extended to include the way young people are disciplined in schools. While we may talk about wanting to engage all students in learning that allows for genuine choices and is structured to meet a variety of learning needs, many educators will not use democratic strategies when correcting the behavior of a bothersome student. Teachers and administrators who have told me they believe in facilitating the learning process for each student seem rarely to include in this the facilitation of appropriate behaviors. All too often, the lofty ideals of democratic education do not see the light of day once teachers and administrators weigh the possibility of losing control as they help young people learn to make responsible decisions about their own comportment.

In 1969, the Supreme Court handed down what is now known as the Tinker decision, a ruling that guaranteed students their citizenship rights in public schools. In his book, *The First Freedom*, Nat Hentoff states: "The decision, *Tinker v. Des Moines Independent School District* is a Magna Carta for all students in this nation. . . . As the *Harvard Law Review* put it, 'The [Supreme] Court adopted the view that the process of education in a democracy must be democratic.' "[1] Despite the fact that Tinker has been the law of the land for over thirty years, the culture of most schools continues to reflect a trend of teaching democracy through a "do as I say, not as I do" approach. Students in public schools, grades K–12, are told, often in trivial detail, what to wear and not to wear, what they can and cannot do, and even when they may or may not attend to the calls of nature, based on schedules that have more to do with arbitrary time slots than with biological need. Commonly, students are stripped of the ability to make decisions concerning their bodies, their habits, and their behaviors while, by means of embarrassment and coercion, they are bent to the will of another's convenience and standards. We call this educating for democracy.

This chapter's intent is to move beyond identifying the problem and to offer an alternative approach, Judicious Discipline, developed by Forrest Gathercoal, which provides a framework for rules and decisions based on constitutional rights as well as citizenship responsibilities.[2] It provides educators with guidelines for

engaging young people in an ongoing exploration of the social con-
tract which, according to de Toqueville, is, or should be, the defin-
ing philosophy of our public education. "It cannot be doubted that
in the United States the instruction of the people powerfully contributed to the support of the democratic republic; and such must
always be the case, I believe, where the instruction which enlight-
ens the understanding is not separated from the moral education
which amends the heart."[3]

Gathercoal's vision for Judicious Discipline is that its legal
language and strategies for teaching rights and responsibilities will
serve as a foundation for democratic classroom practices. It is most
effective when integrated with other strategies for democratic education, such as those recommended by William Glasser, Rudolf
Dreikurs, William Purkey, Thomas Lickona, and Jane Nelsen.[4] These
and other writers have contributed to an ongoing conversation about
the value of democratic education. Each provides a different view
of how to achieve equitable learning communities in public schools.
Educators using Judicious Discipline report that its legal framework has served as a catalyst for integrating democratic practices
into their practice and curriculum.

Teaching Student Rights

Judicious Discipline is designed to teach students about their individual rights, as guaranteed by the United States Constitution,
and how those rights are always balanced against compelling state
interests that protect our society's need for a safe, healthy, and
undisrupted environment. The language used by the Supreme Court
in handing down the Tinker decision, mentioned earlier, clarifies
this basic constitutional precept. John and Mary Beth Tinker, together with a few of their friends, decided to protest the Viet Nam
War by wearing black armbands to their junior and senior high
schools in Des Moines, Iowa, and were subsequently suspended for
their actions. They protested their suspension; eventually, the case
was heard by the United States Supreme Court. The resulting
landmark decision clearly established the rights and responsibilities of students attending public schools in our society. The majority opinion reads in part:

In order for the State in the person of school officials to justify prohibition of a particular expression of opinion, it must be able to show that its action was caused by something more than a mere desire to avoid the discomfort and unpleasantness that always accompany an unpopular viewpoint. Certainly where there is no finding and no showing that engaging in the forbidden conduct would "materially and substantially interfere with the requirements of appropriate discipline in the operation of the school," the prohibition cannot be sustained.[5]

The majority opinion went on to say: "In our system, state-operated schools may not be enclaves of totalitarianism. School officials do not possess absolute authority over their students. Students in school as well as out of school are 'persons' under our Constitution. They are possessed of fundamental rights which the State must respect, just as they themselves must respect their obligations to the State."[6]

Teachers using Judicious Discipline in their classrooms begin the school year by introducing students to some of the wide-ranging implications of the Supreme Court's decision in *Tinker v. Des Moines Independent School District*. Students first learn about the concepts of freedom, justice, and equality based on their rights under the First, Fourth, and Fourteenth Amendments. Very briefly, students are taught that the First Amendment protects the basic nature of who we are, what we say, write, and believe. The Fourth Amendment protects us from unreasonable searches and seizure of our property. The Fourteenth Amendment guarantees our right to Equal Protection under the law, as well as the right to Due Process at the hands of the state. Although *all* citizenship rights are guaranteed to students in public schools, educators typically spend most of their time dealing with issues related to these three amendments, which is why Judicious Discipline makes them a primary focus. During the rest of the year, the concepts of equity and tolerance continue to be emphasized, discussed, and practiced.

Daily Lessons in Citizenship

Judicious Discipline infuses constitutional language and democratic citizenship education into the decision-making processes of the class-

room. Typically, students come into contact with constitutional language only through social studies lessons and civics classes. I
recently visited a fifth grade classroom where the teacher was preparing to introduce Judicious Discipline to her students. As she
was engaged in posting explanations of the First, Fourth, and
Fourteenth Amendments on the bulletin board, her students began
to enter the classroom. "What's that?" they asked, and then answered their own question by saying, "Oh, it's social studies." These
students seemed to think that the words on the bulletin board had
more to do with social studies than with their day-to-day lives. In
contrast, the classrooms I have visited that have been using Judicious Discipline provide students with an ongoing citizenship experience as they interweave constitutional concepts into everyday
interaction among students and between students and teachers. I
have observed students practicing due process in their exchanges
with each other and their teachers. If students in a classroom using
Judicious Discipline feel they are being treated unfairly, they understand that they may appeal the teacher's decision within the
parameters of the appropriate time, place, and manner. I witnessed
one fourth grader, who was upset about some incident that had just
occurred, quietly approach his teacher and request a "conflict conference." The teacher met with him in a corner of the classroom for
a brief period, not more than two minutes, and the matter was
resolved. In this situation, the student's right to due process was
respected by the teacher, while the student carefully observed his
responsibilities of approaching the teacher at the appropriate time
and in the appropriate manner.

Students seem to feel more ownership of an environment that
ensures them their due process. My own research[7] supports unpublished research by C. A. Kelly, cited by David Schimmel and Richard Williams in an article on the use of due process in public
schools. In their review of the literature, Schimmel and Williams
present evidence that "in those schools that observe due process,
students were more likely to have positive attitudes toward the
legal system, and toward schooling."[8]

Beyond due process, however, other basic precepts of the
Constitution find their way into the speech of students experiencing Judicious Discipline. One first grade student responded to
another student who pulled a ribbon out of her hair by saying, "I
have a First Amendment right to wear that ribbon!" She was

demonstrating an early understanding of her personal freedoms and right to expression.

The Other Side of the Balance

I have found that many educators hold the mistaken belief that a democratic classroom is one in which students are permitted to invent their own rules. According to this belief, the teacher asks students what rules they would like to have, the students vote on the rules, and their decisions, whatever they might be, are put in place. While this process of having students create their own rules may seem to be democratic, it typically lacks what Thomas Lickona refers to as an "important connection between school and the wider world."[9] Judicious Discipline uses the United States Constitution to establish this connection, as it attempts to mirror our society by helping students understand that all freedoms are limited by societal expectations. Adults in the United States do not wake up in the morning and invent a new set of laws each day. We accept and adhere to commonly understood limits on our freedoms so that we may each feel secure. All citizens ideally share an understanding that we are free to go about our business each day as long as we do not materially or substantially disrupt those around us.

At developmentally appropriate levels, students in classrooms practicing Judicious Discipline engage in citizenship education by studying and discussing their constitutional rights. However, they are also helped to understand that their rights are only half of the picture. The other half consists of explanation as to when those rights can and should be denied. Our nation's courts have identified four areas of compelling state interest in our public schools, each of which may, in some instances, constrain individual freedom. These areas are:

1. *Property loss and damage*
2. *Legitimate educational purpose*
3. *Health and safety*
4. *Serious disruption of the educational process*

It is important to understand how each compelling state interest has a specific role to play in public schools.

Property loss and damage in a public school would apply to a broad range of rules dealing with everything from proper footwear on the gym floor to care of personal property, desks, lockers, and technical equipment. Students spend a lot of time in public schools and so have many opportunities to damage or take property, intentionally or not. Everyone involved in public schools, from federal officials to the parent who lives a block away, has an interest in seeing that school and personal property is protected. It is important, then, that teachers and administrators take seriously their responsibility to protect the personal belongings and school equipment that occupy school rooms, desks, lockers, and backpacks. Rules must be explicit, fair, and reasonably related to the loss or damage intended to be prevented.

The second compelling state interest, *legitimate educational purpose*, focuses on the curricular aspects of the school day. A teacher's selection of what material will be taught on any given day, rules about bringing supplies and books to class, even state laws concerning compulsory education are all part of legitimate educational purpose. Educators are responsible for carrying out curricular programs consistent with state law. They are considered the experts in matters of academic decisions which include content, assessment, and designing learning opportunities in order to meet a broad range of individual needs.

The *health and safety* of students in a school must be foremost in the thinking of educators and staff. Rules based on this compelling state interest will cover among other topics: the necessity for protective gear on the playing fields and in the technology shop, appropriate ways to move in hallways and classrooms, the need for vaccination and inoculations before attending school, and standards for conduct on the playground. A fundamental purpose of government is to protect the health and welfare of its citizens, and this is especially important when applied to young people who are compelled by law to attend school. Where the implementation of students' rights is likely to lead to student injury, the decision must be in favor of the compelling state interest to protect health and safety.

Finally, students need to understand the issues surrounding what may or may not be a *serious disruption of the educational process*. Guidelines for working individually or within groups, for behaving in various educational settings throughout the school building, and about appropriate language and dress should all be part of the discussion a teacher holds with students in order to clarify these expectations.

However, it is difficult to know what constitutes a serious disruption as opposed to behaviors that are within a student's legitimate exercise of rights. The key to this issue is whether a student's behavior is sufficient to interfere materially and substantially with the opportunity of everyone else to learn. I have observed that educators often define behaviors they have found bothersome as serious disruption. However, irritating mannerisms or behaviors are really not comparable to a disruption that seriously impacts schooling.

For example, some educators believe that students should not have the right to wear hats in school. When I ask them why they have a rule that bans the wearing of hats, they will often say that they want to teach students proper manners. When I respond that removing a hat in certain public places is not an expectation in many of the cultures represented in our public schools, they will acknowledge the truth of that statement and come back with something like, "What if I just don't like it?" They seem not to understand that not liking what others wear does not equate with respecting an individual's First Amendment right to expression. While some teachers might choose to limit First Amendment rights on the basis of "I just don't like it," they would find it difficult to prove that such reasoning reflects true democratic thinking.

The manner in which Judicious Discipline approaches the wearing of hats is a good illustration of how rights and responsibilities can be played out in public schools. First of all, under Judicious Discipline, students would be guaranteed their First Amendment rights to expression, which includes the wearing of hats. The other side of the balance, that of student responsibility, would include a discussion of what to do if a hat were blocking the view of another student, if the hat had writing on it that was vulgar, if the hat were decorated with bangles that made noise when the student's head turned, and when and where hats should be removed.

A growing concern in many schools is what to do about students wearing gang-related attire. In an effort to keep gangs out of schools, some administrators have been known to create a compendium of rules describing in detail what colors, symbols, and brand names of clothing may or may not be worn to school. Those professionals who work closely with youth gangs, though, have told me that gang dress is very fluid. If a school rule is made that bans the wearing of one fashion, gangs will shift to another. In addition, many non-gang affiliated young people are adopting gang-related dress as a personal statement of their own. And, finally, on game day, when the members of the football team all wear their jerseys to class, it can be very difficult to define exactly what is and is not a gang.

The issue with gangs is not the attire but the behaviors. The state's compelling interest in health and safety, as well as its interest in preventing serious disruption, is more than adequate for addressing dangerous behaviors exhibited by any student. Rather than becoming mired in a never-ending attempt to ban the latest gang-related fashion, educators should focus on the overarching concerns of maintaining a productive learning environment in which students can come to and go from school safely. One principal, who was using Judicious Discipline in his inner city high school, suddenly was faced with opposing gang members on campus. His response is indicative of what democratic decision-making and Judicious Discipline are all about. He called off classes for one full day and, instead, held a series of workshops students were expected to attend. The speakers were police officers, youth counselors, former gang members, and other community representatives who provided students with the information needed to make wise decisions. Since that time, the principal has reported no overt gang activity on his school grounds.

Occasionally, teachers will tell me that they justify a "no hats" rule on the grounds that hats cause serious disruption because other students take hats and throw them around. This reasoning is difficult to sustain, however, if we are trying to create a democratic school climate because, in fact, it punishes the victim. In effect, educators who subscribe to this thinking are willing to deny one child his or her constitutional right to freedom of expression in order to prevent the rest of the students from engaging in mob behavior. Judicious Discipline would advocate, instead, that it is the professional responsibility of teachers and administrators to help all the other students understand the value of tolerating one student's individual statement.

Applying the Compelling State Interests

The four compelling state interests described above can inform students about society's expectations for responsible behavior, as well as serve as the framework for classroom and school-wide rules. When teachers and administrators build their learning environment on a foundation of constitutional concepts, they find that students use the language of these concepts to resolve their conflicts. A third grade student who was being chased by bullies to a school bus turned on them, pointed, and said: "You can't do that to me. That's health and safety!" In other words, she was saying to them that all of society didn't want her treated that way. The language of Judicious Discipline not only provides students with a means of resolving conflicts peacefully, it also teaches them that we are not isolated beings but part of a larger whole. The actions of each of us have an effect on all of us.

Judicious Discipline offers students a means of integrating the language of citizenship into every encounter they have with teachers and administrators, and with their peers. Students learn a language of civility with which to communicate their individual feelings, yet understand when their interests must yield to the welfare of others. This new language and rationale for civil behavior forms the basis of the democratic culture pervading a classroom or school practicing Judicious Discipline.

As I indicated above, students quickly pick up and apply the language of citizenship once they have experienced it. When I interview students and ask them to explain to me what Judicious Discipline is, they respond with something like: "It's your rights and responsibilities." Or, "It's the balance of how you get along in our country." I have never had students describe it to me as an opportunity to do whatever they want. But they do find that it provides them with a language that reflects our country's balance of social responsibilities and individual liberties.

And When a Rule Is Broken . . .

When they mete out punishments to students, adults are imposing solutions for the problems presented to them and so are assuming responsibility for the situations. Students merely have to accept whatever decisions are doled out and acquiesce for the time stipulated by the adult, or not, in which case students typically leave school and learn the lessons of life in other settings. That punishment will effectively solve behavior problems makes sense to many teachers and administrators; the desire to lecture and seek retribution becomes almost overwhelming when they face any real or supposed challenge to their authority.

In contrast to the use of punishment, Gathercoal, like Rudolf Dreikurs and William Glasser, among others, favors the use of problem-solving strategies when working through a difficult situation with a student. More common to classroom discipline today is the use of behavioral strategies designed to reward appropriate action and punish those deemed to be inappropriate. John Dewey's response to this form of discipline sets out the philosophical underpinnings Gathercoal has used for Judicious Discipline, when he states:

> To isolate the formal relationship of citizenship from the whole system of relations with which it is actually interwoven; to suppose that there is some one particular study or mode of treatment which can make a child a good citizen; to suppose, in other words, that a good citizen is anything more than a thoroughly efficient and serviceable member of society, one with all his powers of body and mind under control, is a hampering superstition which it is hoped may soon disappear from educational discussion.[10]

Punishing students for inappropriate behavior may seem to be a reasonable course of action until some thought is given to the source of many of the problems acted out in our schools. Often, meting out punishment can mean that educators are seeking retribution from students for home situations that are beyond the control of either group. As a result, punitive measures can result in students becoming angry, frustrated, and ultimately counterproductive members of their learning environments.

Initially, however, punishment may seem to make the problem disappear. The student feels intimidated into working or, just as likely, into leaving school. However, punishment provides only a bandage approach to the misbehaviors exhibited by students. According to Schrag and Divoky, "Behavior modification, by whatever means, is concerned only with behavior, and not with internal states, ailments, diagnoses or etiology."[11] Democratic problem-solving, on the other hand, offers educators a variety of diagnostic strategies to help fix the problem, while maintaining a relationship of trust between student and teacher.

Judicious Discipline places its emphasis on the concept that it is an educator's professional responsibility to work with all students and to explore a variety of problem-solving techniques to help them succeed in school. Rather than creating an arbitary set of consequences that might be applied to any number of inappropriate behaviors, Forrest Gathercoal advocates approaching discipline problems as teachable moments. What does the student need to learn in order to avoid repeating the inappropriate behavior next time? What information does the teacher need to offer that will help the student correct the problem? Gathercoal responds to these questions by stating: "An educator's approach to shaping consequences should reflect the basic principles of empowerment and student responsibility.... Students should know that when rules have been broken, their discussion with educators will center around two important future aspects: (1) What needs to be done? and (2) What needs to be learned?"[12]

In other words, when a student breaks a rule, a teacher who is using Judicious Discipline does not think what punishment should be imposed on this individual so he or she will feel shamed, and never, ever, do whatever it was again. Rather than punishing or embarrassing a student into submission, a judicious educator would take steps to discover the underlying causes of the problem and help the student to develop strategies for solving it. As a teacher stated recently to me: "The focus has shifted from what was the offense and what was the consequence to what does the student need to do to get on with being successful in school." Ultimately, the goal of Judicious Discipline is to create responsible, capable, adult citizens who are empowered with information to make decisions that are helpful to themselves and not intrusive upon the needs of others.

This flexible and creative approach to working through difficult situations encourages educators to draw upon their experience and professional knowledge in order to mentor students. The emphasis is on respecting the right students have to an education, and exhausting every effort to keep them in school. While some students may require alternative settings, and some students may need a short time away from school, Judicious Discipline places its focus on retaining students in their classes.

Practicing Democratic Discipline

By providing a framework for school and classroom rules based on our nation's laws, Judicious Discipline allows educators to overcome the dichotomy between educational settings and society at large. Opportunities to experience citizenship rights as well as the needs and demands of social responsibility help students to experience the self-empowerment that accompanies learning to govern and think for themselves. As one teacher stated, "The children have the opportunity to learn what their rights are as citizens and the responsibilities that go with these rights—balancing freedom and order."

Since the days of Aristotle, education has been viewed as a primary source for passing on the precepts of democratic citizenship. Judicious Discipline suggests that educators now take that belief one step further, to accept and treat students as citizens, thereby creating a democratic setting in our schools that mirrors the same system of laws under which students will live when their compulsory schooling is completed. Educators who have adopted this approach to discipline find that it allows, and indeed encourages, students to experience the joys and sorrows of being accountable for their own actions.

As students develop their paradigms for responsible citizenship, they reveal in conversations their growth and understanding of constitutional expectations. Interviews I have conducted with students often reveal their growing awareness of the role they play in our larger society. For instance, I conducted the following interviews in a ninth grade classroom.

Q. How did Mr. ****** go about setting up rules in this classroom?

A. He didn't.

Q. You just started the school year without rules?

A. (from all four students) Well, wait a minute. He talked about a scale, weights on both sides of the scale.

Q. What did the scale represent?

A. (From one student) The overall welfare of society.
(From another student) It was the rights of the people, rights of the individual.
(From another student) The rules balance out . . . the majority and one person.
[Rules] make them equal.

An interview with another student in the same class:

Q. What was the balance scale all about?

A. We feel equal.

Q. How do you feel equal?

A. We're self-governed. We don't get away with anything major . . . but he knows we're mature enough to know when we're doing something wrong.

Working with Educators

I have worked with Forrest Gathercoal supporting the development of Judicious Discipline through the quantitative as well as qualitative research I have been conducting. As a teacher in the area of classroom discipline as well as a researcher, I was pleased to have the opportunity to assist in the development of a new concept and to help teachers implement it. In addition, my research has taught me a great deal about what teachers do and do not know about our system of government. For two years, I presented inservice sessions on Judicious Discipline in various locations around the United States. I began these sessions with a pretest that asked the educators in attendance what rights are included in the First, Fourth, and Fourteenth Amendments. I also asked them to define "compelling state interest." Workshop participants would typically write the word "speech" under the First Amendment, and, for the majority, that seemed to exhaust their knowledge of the topic. On rare occasions, one participant would know that the

Fourteenth Amendment had to do with due process. This was such a consistent pattern that I have become concerned about how well teachers can pass along democratic values when the random sample with whom I have worked clearly lacked knowledge of our governmental system.

I have discovered, also, that the fundamental concepts of constitutional rights and responsibilities, so elemental to the structure of our democratic society, are the very concepts many educators have trouble understanding and practicing. When I speak to educators about Judicious Discipline, whether it be in inservice seminars, workshops, or classes, they will often express fear and frustration as to the possible outcomes of teaching young people about their citizenship rights. I have found that educators typically can understand the idea of student rights, at least in the abstract, but often fear that if young people really are allowed to make decisions about their own behaviors the inevitable result will be chaos in schools, with students running riot, while their constitutional rights protect them from any consequences to their actions.

On the other hand, educators usually have no trouble understanding or teaching rules that deal with the limitations to student rights. Students' speech, dress, and other forms of expression are so routinely limited to reflect the biases of various communities, that educators and parents alike seem to view this as "the way things ought to be." School rules are designed to enforce the side of the balance that represents responsibility without providing information for students about their rights. The concerns teachers and administrators seem to share in regard to the issue of student rights are reflected in the comment one teacher made to me: "Can't I just teach them about their responsibilities? Do I have to also teach them their rights?" However, it is the balance between the two that defines our entire system of government. We must ask ourselves if students are being well prepared to assume their roles as productive, responsible citizens if those charged with passing on such information are the very same people who appear either to not understand it or to be afraid of its implications.

In my conversations with teachers and administrators, I have learned that two issues, the wearing of hats and the chewing of gum—issues that reflect common applications of or limitations to student rights—create a great deal of consternation among them. I am continually surprised at the time educators will spend and the lengths to which they will go in order to control the wearing of hats and the chewing of gum. Students doing either have been thrown out of classes, made to stand with their noses against the blackboard, made to wear gum on their noses, and have even been suspended from school. Ultimately, the concern teachers and administrators express over these issues seems to boil down to who will be in charge. It is control or the lack thereof that has so many educators heavily invested in eradicating behaviors that otherwise seem trivial.

Judicious Discipline and Assessment

When I work with teachers and administrators who are considering implementing Judicious Discipline, often the topic that brings out the greatest concern is the emphasis Judicious Discipline places on separating academic grades from behavioral information. According to Gathercoal, "it is important to incorporate in the academic grade only those requirements and standards commonly understood by 'the profession' or the community at large to be course content. . . . The liberty issue lies not in what the grade means to the teacher or the student, but that it *communicates to the reader* an accurate statement of the student's academic achievement."[13] [Emphasis in original.]

When I suggest to educators that students should be assessed on their academic understanding of subject material, and that behavioral issues might be recorded as part of anecdotal records, they ask me if it isn't their job to prepare students for the real world, and whether the use of grades to control behavior isn't a good way to get young people used to the tougher side of reality. The Fourteenth Amendment's Due Process clause, however, protects our futures as well as our current lives. Yet these protections for our future expectations are apparently misunderstood by teachers or, more often, are not even considered as relevant when it comes to assessing students' behavior.

Teachers hearing of Judicious Discipline's alternative approaches to assessment, such as separating academic performance from behavioral issues, typically will look at me, pause a moment to consider, and then say: "Yes, but this person is going to have to meet deadlines and show up for work on time at some point.

Shouldn't we be teaching lessons about how to do that?" The idea that punishment and lowered grades are the motivating factors for becoming responsible adults appears to be widely held. I hear that argument from teachers and administrators across the country. The idea that students might feel genuinely motivated to do work without being threatened is something they find almost impossible to believe.

Although educators are among the first to recognize that students often come from homes that are not supportive environments for showing up at school, showing up on time, and showing up with homework completed, some teachers still want to punish a student for failure to do any of these things. One teacher I heard of recently told her students to stand up on their chairs. While they were standing there, she began to read the names of those who did their homework the night before. As soon as a student's name was read, he or she could sit down. One by one the students sat down until four were left standing for all to see. Despite the fact that this teacher is cognizant of all the reasons why homework might be incomplete, she nevertheless seized upon this opportunity to teach a lesson to those who had not done it, through public humiliation, violating all vestiges of student confidentiality.

And so, it seems to me, the question of what discipline practices will be followed boils down to one question, "What is your core belief about students?" If educators believe students to be inherently bad, then tough rules, harsh consequences, and the inevitable suspensions and expulsions make sense. If educators can just get rid of all the bad kids they will be left only with those who are worthy of instruction. The other perspective is that students are inherently good and that even good kids can get into trouble when faced with the myriad of problems that pervade our society today. Educators who favor the latter perspective work hard to keep students in what may be for many the only safe and structured environment they ever know, the public school.

The Experiences of Teachers and Administrators

Some teachers and administrators skeptically consider the concepts of Judicious Discipline and say: "It can't be that easy." So, let me share with you some of the findings I have gathered from observations, surveys, and interviews with students and teachers who are experiencing Judicious Discipline together. The model is currently being used in schools across the country, in grades K through 12, in rural, urban, and suburban settings. It is also being used as a whole-school model, as well as in individual classrooms. The response by teachers and administrators who implement most or all aspects of Judicious Discipline is overwhelmingly favorable. On a school-wide basis, in all settings, typically the first change is a reduction in office referrals. In interviews I have conducted, educators report feeling more confident about their decisions, because the language they use with students is legal, fair, and rational. Hence they are more willing to solve problems in their classrooms and not seek outside interventions. A principal noted that some teachers had developed strategies for keeping students in class, such as "giving students five minutes to talk but expecting quiet and attention the rest of the time. Also an attitude of trying to keep students in class longer rather than expecting them to be permanently removed."

Attendance rates tend to increase with Judicious Discipline. Students report that they see the schools as safer places to be, which may help account for the increase. One urban high school found that it had to accommodate to a daily absence rate that went from fifteen percent to three percent after implementing Judicious Discipline. The principal told me that he now had to figure out where to put all the students who were attending regularly.

Schools tend to experience a greater sense of calm. One principal of a small rural elementary school using Judicious Discipline reported to me that no students were being sent to her office during those typically difficult months of April and May. She thought perhaps her teachers were trying to spare her extra work, but when she asked, she was told there just weren't any problems. Another elementary school principal stated: "Judicious Discipline has given our staff a democratic framework on which to base our school's discipline philosophy, policies, and practices. It empowers us to be educators as opposed to disciplinarians when responding to student problems. Our focus is now on what the child needs to learn in order to improve and be successful at school, rather than on punishment for a misbehavior.[14]

High schools report fewer suspensions, in part because the schools are making the effort to exercise options that will help to correct problems while keeping students in school. A common alternative to suspension is a form of in-school suspension that places students in a tutorial setting with adults who are there to help with work and provide counseling as needed. One resource for staffing these settings is senior citizen volunteers.

While some teachers move swiftly to alter their classrooms, others adopt Judicious Discipline more slowly. Some teachers restructure their classroom rules to reflect the compelling state interests, while others simply begin to use the language of the constitutional balance when working through behavioral problems with students.

One frequent first step is issuing receipts when confiscating a toy or other property from a student. The practice of using receipts is another example of how the constitutional balance can be applied in the classroom. A student has the right to have his or her property treated with respect, as opposed to being arbitrarily confiscated. On the other hand, students cannot use their property to disrupt the learning environment. When a student's toy or other item is used to cause a serious disruption, a teacher may confiscate it. Judicious Discipline provides ideas for taking the item in a manner that demonstrates respect for democratic processes as well as the student. The teacher gives the student a receipt for the item, and then makes sure the item is stored in a safe place until it is reclaimed. Later that day, or at the end of the period, a student can bring the receipt back and have the item returned. This process seems almost insignificant in its simplicity, and yet it will often prove to be the one act that convinces teachers they are on the right track in using Judicious Discipline.

The receipt stories I have heard are numerous, and I will share only a couple here. One middle-school teacher, after hearing about receipts, decided to try them. The next week he shared this story with Forrest Gathercoal. A student walked into his first period class with a bag of sunflower seeds. The teacher asked the student to bring them to his desk. Ordinarily the teacher would have thrown them out, but this time he picked up a pad of paper and a pen and said, "Just a minute, I'm going to write you a receipt." He quickly scribbled one out and handed it to the student, saying, "Bring that to me at the end of the period and you can have the sunflower seeds back." The student laughed, held the receipt up in the air and said "Look what I got." On his way back to his desk, he was laughing, and soon had all the other students laughing as well. The teacher's hands grew sweaty as he thought "What have I done?" But when the student sat down again and the laughter subsided, all eyes turned back to the teacher. He later recounted, "In fifteen years of teaching, that was the single most significant thing I have done. I have never seen such respect in the eyes of students before. Just because I had shown respect for a package of sunflower seeds."

A second grade teacher was about to issue her first receipt, but the student didn't want to give up the toy. Another student walked up and said, "Relax! She's going to give you a receipt." She said to me that she was really surprised that something so simple could have such a powerful effect.

Of course, as the constitutional balance is applied, issuing receipts in order to confiscate and safely return property would not be appropriate if the item to be confiscated presented a clear and present danger to the rest of the student population. If the item to be confiscated were not dangerous, but questionable, teachers could use their professional discretion in deciding how to handle the situation. For instance, a third grade student brings an issue of *Hustler* magazine to school. It is not a dangerous item but it may not be appropriate to return it to the student. It may be a wiser decision to call the parents or guardians before or instead of releasing the item to the student at the end of the day.

Implications for Teacher Education

That there is a need for citizenship education is undoubtable. That democratic education should be infused in schools is a concept to which we all pay tribute. As Alfie Kohn wrote: "I believe it is time to call the bluff of every educator who claims to prize democratic principles. Anyone who truly values democracy ought to be thinking about preparing students to participate in a democratic culture—or to transform a culture into a democracy."[15]

However, when push comes to shove, the issue of democratic schooling comes home to the doorstep of teacher education programs and the model they present of how children should be educated. If we believe we are training teachers to be both respectful of individual needs and focused on fostering democracy, then our actions and deeds with our own students must be fashioned as a mirror of these goals. As teacher educators, we have to be willing to ask ourselves not how thoroughly we discuss democratic principles in our programs but rather how completely we model them in our syllabi, our grading practices, and our willingness to encourage our students to make decisions concerning their own learning.

Oregon State University's Elementary Education portion of the Professional Teacher Education program continually strives to find ways to model democratic processes in education, in the hope that if our students live it they will be more likely to practice it in their own classrooms. Members of the Elementary Education faculty do not include attendance or participation in the criteria for course assessments. Our students attend classes because it is important and meaningful for them to do so, not because they are intimidated into it. If some take advantage of what seems to them a lenient policy, we call the students in for advising sessions and work together to find a solution. Judicious Discipline helps us to resist nagging these students into appropriate behaviors, and to focus on issues of professionalism. We also hold class meetings to discuss these issues. While we assign due dates for administrative convenience, late work is listed as incomplete until it comes in. The elementary education faculty at Oregon State University has decided that our policies will reflect our shared belief that it is more important to help students become good teachers than to pressure them into doing less than their best work in order to meet an arbitrary deadline.

We also strive to provide our students with choices over their learning opportunities. Students have genuine input into the program through their journal entries and the class meetings we hold on a regular basis. While certain elements of our program cannot be open to negotiation, there is room for flexibility within the general framework.

During our Winter term, we provide students with the opportunity to determine for themselves what would be the most beneficial learning options for each of them. We let them know that they are responsible for sixty hours of course work. Then we provide for them a smorgasbord of workshops, much the same as they would experience at a conference, and from which they can pick and choose. They also have the option of forming reading groups that meet independently to discuss some piece of literature they are reading together. Or they can design an independent project they want to pursue.

In their Classroom Management course, our students video-tape themselves, analyze the tape with the use of a checklist of basic student-centered management strategies, and then set their own personal goals for the course, based on what they believe to be areas in which they need improvement. As their instructor, I also view their tapes and have the option of suggesting additional goals to them. For instance, if a student were unable to establish any goal, I could meet with that student, we could review the tape together, and I could offer suggestions as to what might need atten-tion. Giving students genuine choices and support does not equate with a lessening of my professional responsibilities as their educa-tor, but rather works toward our creating a partnership approach to learning.

Finally, our students exit our program on the basis of a pro-fessional portfolio they assemble over the course of their fifth year. Students often comment to us that one of the most significant aspects of our program to them is that we model what we teach. While that is gratifying, it is also sad that many students tell us it is the first time they have experienced that in their educational careers.

Conclusion

Judicious Discipline begins with an educator's belief that all stu-dents have value and, with guidance, are capable of appropriate social interaction. While it is important to establish the boundaries necessary for a positive educational atmosphere, I believe it is equally important to communicate to students that they are an integral part of the school environment and their opinions are worthwhile. I can attest that the application of more than two hundred years' worth of constitutional wisdom and authority, prop-erly presented and discussed, can work wonders for teachers and administrators seeking to bring about a school climate of mutual regard and respect.

If schools are indeed laboratories of democracy then it only makes sense that the disciplinary system in schools also reflect democratic principles. In our larger society, we are faced on a daily basis with the challenges that tolerance, personal responsibility, and acceptance can bring. Nevertheless, some schools use authoritarian strategies to push erring students out, even though our larger society is trying to find ways to include, or at least afford due process to, all who come here. Can we say that we lift the lamp beside the golden door only to snuff it out at the schoolhouse gate? While it is easy to promote democracy as an ideal educational model, it is apparently much more difficult for educators to be willing to create a school environment in which students can live and experience democracy throughout the day, in every aspect of their education. Judicious Discipline offers educators a framework and strategies to help them turn the ideal into a day-by-day reality.

NOTES

1. Nat Hentoff, *The First Freedom* (New York: Delacorte Press, 1980), p. 5.

2. See Forrest Gathercoal, *Judicious Discipline* (Ann Arbor: Caddo Gap Press, 1990).

3. Alexis de Tocqueville, *Democracy in America* (New York: Alfred A. Knopf, Inc., 1945. [Originally published 1848]), p. 329.

4. See William Glasser, *Schools Without Failure* (New York: Harper and Row, 1969), and *Control Theory in the Classroom* (New York: Harper and Row, 1986); Rudolf Dreikurs, *Maintaining Sanity in the Classroom: Classroom Management Techniques* (New York: Harper and Row, 1982); William W. Purkey and D. Strahan, *Positive Discipline: A Pocketful of Ideas* (Columbus, Ohio: National Middle School Association, 1989); Thomas Lickona, *Educating for Character* (New York: Bantam Books, 1992); and Jane Nelsen, *Positive Discipline* (New York: Ballantine Books, 1987).

5. *Tinker v. Des Moines Independent School District*, Supreme Court of the United States, 1969, 393 U. S. 503, as cited in Michael W. LaMorte, *School Law: Cases and Concepts*, 4th. ed. (Needham Heights, Mass.: Allyn and Bacon, 1993).

6. *Tinker v. Des Moines Independent School District*, 1969.

7. Barbara McEwan, "Democratic Practices in Grades K–12: An Investigation of the Practical Applications of Judicious Discipline in Public School Classrooms." An ongoing study. Quotations throughout the chapter

from my own interviews with students, teachers, and administrators are from this study.

8. David Schimmel and Richard Williams, "Does Due Process Interfere with School Discipline?", *High School Journal* 68, no. 2 (December 1984 to January 1985): 47–51. Schimmel and Williams cite: C. A. Kelly, "Due Process in the Schools, the View from Inside," Unpublished doctoral dissertation, Northwestern University, 1979.

9. Lickona, *Educating for Character,* p. 114.

10. John Dewey, *Philosophy of Education* (Ames, Iowa: Littlefield, Adams and Co., 1956. [Originally published as *Problems of Men* (Philosophical Library, Inc., 1946)]), p. 49.

11. Peter Schrag and Diane Divoky, *The Myth of the Hyperactive Child and Other Means of Child Control* (New York: Random House, 1975), chapter entitled "Therapy, Punishment, Control." [Reprinted in: Jerome H. Skolnick and Elliott Currie, eds., *Crisis in American Institutions*, 4th ed. (New York: Little, Brown and Company, 1976)].

12. Gathercoal, *Judicious Discipline*, 3rd ed., p. 117.

13. Gathercoal, *Judicious Discipline*, 3rd. ed., p. 140.

14. McEwan, "Democratic Practices in Grades K–12," ongoing study.

15. Alfie Kohn, "Choices for Children: Why and How to Let Students Decide," *Phi Delta Kappan* 75, no. 1 (September 1993): 20.

Donald Warren

Chapter 7

✧

Practice Makes Perfect:
Civic Education
by Precept and Example

Introduction

All citizens of the United States, by definition, play active political roles. To refrain from action, by not voting, for example, remains a form of action. Good citizens, on the other hand, by longstanding agreement within the public discourse on American political responsibilities, are informed participants.[1] They seek evidence, analyze issues, devote time to civic duties, and demonstrate willingness to defer self and immediate interests to achieve common and long-term welfare. They are familiar with basic democratic concepts, endorse democratic ideals, and consent to be governed according to the ratified documents that organize and distribute political power. The traditional rationale for civic education in the United States has rested on the necessity of such citizens to the health and growth of the republic.

One could argue that civic instruction in any society occurs inevitably as a function of experience. People learn their proper roles through interactions in multiple settings—workplaces, homes, religious gatherings, theaters, and schools, to illustrate the point—although the lessons thus acquired may not be the ones intended. Unwilling to leave such matters to chance, governments with differing political bents have devised formal preparation programs intended to deflect or channel political participation and promote patriotism. But political socialization alone cannot satisfy the goals of civic education in a society like the United States. The purposes have been not merely to maintain a status quo but to widen social membership by enlightening successive generations of the young and the newcomers who came in seemingly endless waves of immigration. More fundamentally, the goals have reflected confidence in the mutability of people and the renewability of national principles and ideals. Not surprisingly, the curricula of school-based civic education have tended to emphasize history, the point being to keep the preparation of U.S. citizens earthbound by recalling the origins of democratic values and the extent to which confidence in them has been rewarded or betrayed, and why.

Civic Education and the Public School

As B. Edward McClellan has noted, the preparation of citizens in the United States has represented a subset of moral education.[2] Both have been propelled by similar and overlapping goals, and in

121

some periods the two efforts have been indistinguishable. While both have assumed a standard of exemplary behavior, practical concern about the country's need for responsible citizens has tended to focus on demographic conditions and worry about maintaining national stability, not on the need for people to learn about abstract political ideals. The latter have typically been invoked only when national stability appeared to some as endangered. At the turn of the nineteenth century, however, France represented to many Americans a disturbing example of a new republic in which political change spun out of control and democratic ideals lost their hold on the public conscience. The lesson seemed clear: democratic citizens are made, not born. Without educational preparation, they are at risk of squandering their political birthright. The lesson acquired special meaning in the United States because of the roles immigrants had played in forming the nation.

The founding leaders saw two sorts of educational issues in connection with their concerns about the union's permanence and domestic peace. One had to do with the fact of independence and the republican form of government, the other with the diversity of the American people. The Revolutionary War had not attracted unanimous support among the colonists, and by some counts roughly one-third had remained apathetic. Benjamin Rush, for one, fretted about transforming citizens under the old regime into "republican machines," individuals who practiced the new political habits needed to secure the nation's future.[3] The problem was that governmental structures and political institutions at local, state, and national levels had to be modified or invented. These tasks, according to Rush, required literate, thoughtful, and loyal citizens, and thus, planned approaches to education. Although the idea failed to strike a popular chord, other leaders during the early national period agreed, and several of them authored proposals for national and state school systems intended specifically to prepare citizens for service to the republic.[4]

Acknowledging the United States' diversity and its continued dependence on England and other European countries, Noah Webster devised educational strategies to foster New World loyalties and deference to American heroes.[5] George Washington decried sectionalism, advocating "the assimilation of the principles, opinions, and manners of our countrymen . . . from every quarter. . . . The more homogeneous our citizens can be made in these particulars the greater will be our prospect of permanent union."[6] He thought national educational institutions would advance the cause. Taking a different tack, Thomas Jefferson envisioned improved systems of transportation, trade, communication, education, and other internal improvements to blur the "lines of separation."[7] These early discussions of citizenship revealed contradictory longings. The taste of independence remained new and sweet but threats of unbridled individuality and separatist leanings among the states suggested the necessity of caution. For many, "e pluribus unum" required at least a modicum of conformity among citizens so different among themselves and so recently liberated.

The need for self-restraint, as a balance to social reform, arose not merely from the falling away of colonial institutions, and the concomitant rise of new ones, but from dramatic political, economic, and demographic changes during the first decades of the nineteenth century. Extensions of the franchise in most states to essentially all adults who were both white and male brought new voters to the polls and, in 1829, Andrew Jackson to the White House. Immigration continued to add to the young nation's diversity. City populations swelled, not merely with foreigners but also with those crowding in from farming areas. A foreboding development to the Protestant majority was the arrival in great numbers of impoverished Roman Catholic Irish. These changes coincided with emerging industrial modes of production that altered working conditions, shifted employment opportunities from craftspeople to unskilled laborers, and introduced unprecedented strains on the family, which in pre-industrial times had functioned as more of an economic unit. As a speaker to a gathering of educators in 1837 put it, "All the elements of society are in commotion. . . . Moral revolution—moral chaos—seems approaching."[8]

Given the commotion, it is not surprising that reform passion blossomed during the 1830s and 1840s. Women's rights, peace, temperance, slavery, labor unions, and education all rallied advocates and organizations. These movements, with their cross-cutting aims and overlapping memberships, adopted similar strategies of exhortation and institution-building. The aims were to shape individual character and to fashion social structures that would reinforce self-discipline and personal resolve. The point was more to reform people than society. An emerging consensus assigned the task to systems of common schools.

In the Foreword to David Bricker, *Classroom Life as Civic Education*, Kenneth Strike comments on the "reciprocal relation" between schools as institutions and the formation of students' character.[9] He concedes that this powerful interaction, unanchored in the literature of democratic thought, often remains unarticulated and thus forms part of the hidden curriculum. Americans in the late twentieth century, he observes, "have lost touch with too much of our political heritage. We lack the concepts with which to see."[10] Those who originated the common school meant to create an institution that in all its aspects, not merely through its curriculum, would function as civic educator, and as a conduit of knowledge about the nation's political heritage.

Governor William H. Seward saw the connection between schooling and citizenship as so obvious it required no elaboration. In 1839, his primary concern was with the number of children in New York who lacked access to a school.[11] For Henry Barnard, common schools promised "proper preparation for the real business of life": citizenship, work, individual autonomy, and social membership.[12] However inadequately financed and staffed, common schools could achieve such results primarily because of the uniquely American political and economic context in which they functioned. European countries could also boast of general schooling opportunities, but their efforts were "depressed" by entrenched custom and "repressive despotic government."[13] In the United States, the free press, voting rights, and individual liberty reinforced the civic goals of schools. Hiram H. Barney, in 1854 the first Ohio commissioner of common schools, voiced the claim asserted by political and educational leaders across the northern states. Educate every child to the highest level possible, he promised, and you bestow on the community "productive artisans, good citizens, upright jurors and magistrates," and dispensers of virtue.[14]

The common school proponents came of age in a time of social and intellectual unrest. For that reason, perhaps, they sought an institution that would serve as a stabilizing influence. Horace Mann's biographer concluded that this intention best explained Mann's elaborate, if hyperbolic, vision of the school's communitarian role.[15] With the breakdown of the pre-industrial socializing nexus formed by family, church, and village mores, Mann sought a replacement, an enabling institution to supply the means for shaping the character and sensibilities of the young. Systems of common schools would constitute this powerful and empowering social structure.

Although the language in which it was couched has been ridiculed, and the goal of political empowerment doubted, Mann's vision of the common school as civic educator advocated more than a general diffusion of elementary knowledge. Of course, he conceded, the people must be literate. Otherwise, the "splendid structure" devised by the nation's founders would fall into the hands of those incapable "of reading one word of the language which describes its framework" and its history.[16] Ignorant voters limited candidates to a single way of presenting themselves—from the stump. Politicians could not publish their views with any hope the voters would consider them. Furthermore, to attract attention, orations had to be delivered at full throttle. "Stump-speaking," in Mann's view, prevailed in proportion to the voters' inability to read, and it reached demagogic excesses as the issues became more complex. According to Mann, voting required abilities to probe the character and wisdom of potential leaders, analyze social problems, and weigh the effects of policies on present and future generations. It entailed far more than casting ballots. To meet their various responsibilities, citizens must be capable of independence, because the dependent were prone to act from malice, envy, or wantonness, or against their own judgments through fear or bribery. In short, the United States, this "great experiment of republicanism," tested the people's capacity for self-government.[17]

Mann knew that many of his contemporaries, fearing the horde, favored a narrow dissemination of power to those defined as superior, and he sought to broaden their view. He also intended to contest widely held notions of original sin, which rendered any educational initiative hopeless from the start. Success would "spring from a belief in the goodness of God and the progressive happiness of man."[18] The nation needed informed citizens, surely, but it needed even more those whose "vitality . . . burst forth spontaneously into action."[19] It needed citizens of general intelligence and integrity.

Bringing these "germs" of ability into full flower was a policy matter of the utmost importance. The necessity of schools rested on this imperative, not schools for the select few but for all, not academies and colleges but common schools. These institutions, Mann thought, would inculcate belief in "native, inborn equality . . . practically . . . by their being open to all, good enough for all, and attended by all."[20] In 1842, this was his way of underscoring the ineluctable relation of educational excellence and equity in any democratic society that aspired to flourish. Robert Dale Owen used similar language in arguing that public education in the United States ought "to be equal, republican, open to all, and the best which can be devised."[21] A sharp critic of common schools, Owen viewed them as pale shadows of the radical liberation that citizens of democratic society required. He joined, however, in expecting the public school to function as the nation's democratic cradle.

Other well-known advocates endorsed Mann's reform goals but not his democratic beliefs. Henry Barnard, Mann's widely respected contemporary, who, in the 1840s, led the common school effort in Connecticut and Rhode Island, held more restrictive views on equality. He abhorred slavery, but contrary to Mann, accepted the southern position on the abolitionist movement. For Barnard, abolitionism raised more questions about property rights than about morality and individual liberty.[22] Noah Webster, whose ubiquitous "speller" schooled countless generations in standard English and Protestant values, recanted in old age his Jeffersonian sins, angrily denouncing republican equality as impossible to attain and in any case undesirable.[23]

Beneath the quarrels, all tended to agree that the common school as an invented system, spread across the land, could bring national unity, promote political morality, diminish crime and vice, and equip the young to negotiate the currents of social change. The claims were fantastic. Some reflected sheer calculation, an attempt to win popular support for schools by projecting effects likely to calm an anxious public. Mixed in as well were rhetorical excess, certainly in Mann's case, and a dawning awareness that social, economic, and political change placed democratic ideals at risk. Whatever the push and tug of motives, the early advocates of common schooling rarely admitted exceptions of race, ethnicity, social class, or gender in their practical vision of educational inclusiveness.[24] In Mann's words, the country's welfare and its reliance on responsible citizens demanded a public education that was "open to all, good enough for all, and attended by all."[25]

That various motives and forces were at work can be easily seen. Whatever the educational objectives—to prepare a cooperative work force, inculcate common political values, enable student progress toward moral and intellectual independence, or merely equip future citizens with elementary knowledge and cognitive skills—justification of this burgeoning system rested on something like Horace Mann's notion of excellence and equality: the same high level schooling for everyone.

Curricula, Teachers, and Unplanned Civics Lessons

The highminded goals originally assigned to public schools linked the institutions' educational and civic roles. The point has been underscored during two centuries of argument on the necessity of preparing citizens for their responsibilities. Education, equal and exacting, offered the surest guarantee of success. In practice, however, schools fell short of ideal expectations. The gap between rhetoric and reality, while not surprising, has helped explain the repetitious quality of public discourse on civic education over the years.

Blatant and subtle discrepancies appeared almost from the start. During the antebellum period, Roman Catholic children confronted Protestant versions of the Bible embedded in the curriculum. Their history textbooks contained anti-Catholic messages and omitted accounts of violence committed against Catholic neighborhoods and institutions.[26] Study materials were sanitized in other ways, too. Horace Mann, for example, preferred textbooks and school library books that accentuated the positive. He selected works by the best American writers for common school libraries in Massachusetts, but he thought they should portray unity, not diversity, high ideals, not distressing realities. To be useful in common schools, most fiction, in his view, required careful editing, with moral lessons inserted at appropriate points. When he suggested such "slight modification" of *Two Years Before the Mast,* Richard Henry Dana, Jr., thought him "a school master gone crazy."[27] Apparently, Mann did not see his own effort at text modification as contradictory to the goal of preparing citizens who were capable of independent thought and action.

Numerous critics and observers, John Dewey being perhaps the best known, have called attention to the dysfunctional learnings acquired by students from school curricula that subverted democratic ideals, if only tacitly.[28] A recent contributor to this literature, David Bricker has examined how teachers and classrooms shape students' values. He argues that students can be more effectively prepared for their roles as citizens in a democratic society when pedagogies and classroom organization encourage them to practice such social virtues as friendliness, cooperation, and generosity. They learn to be the critical thinkers that democratic society needs by honing their intellectual skills through the give and take of classroom discussion and inquiry.[29] One does not have to accept Bricker's specific recommendations regarding cooperative learning to agree with his basic point. Students acquire lessons in citizenship, perhaps indelibly, from the ways and settings in which they are taught.

Recent assessments of student achievement in social studies have emphasized cognitive development as the principal goal of civic education.[30] American students in the late twentieth century apparently are not well informed about governmental roles and functions in the United States. They have trouble identifying their political leaders, describing how federal or state laws are enacted, or recalling major events in the nation's political history. Typically, they lack detailed knowledge of the United States Constitution and cannot recognize once well-known passages from the Declaration of Independence. As Judith Torney-Purta and her colleagues have found, American students are not alone in their relatively low levels of civic learning. International assessments have reached similar conclusions about students in other countries.

Opinion and attitudinal surveys have gathered equally troubling data on the civic values espoused by contemporary students and on their interest in political participation.[31] High school and college students seem to be more committed to personal goals and material rewards than to social concerns. They demonstrate limited understanding of democratic values and admit to feeling unconstrained by the canons governing democratic processes. On the other hand, they are responsive to political slogans and real or imagined threats to national honor. Such findings raise the spectre of uninformed and disengaged citizens that had worried Horace Mann and his contemporaries. But whether alienated and ill-prepared students can be reclaimed by means of course content in social studies remains unclear.

The evidence tends to support Bricker's provocative finding. A civic education that intends to prepare students for their roles in a democratic society cannot be assigned to the exclusive province of specialized teachers or one segment of the curriculum. To be sure, students can acquire knowledge about systems and institutions of government by taking courses on those topics. This is the traditional mode of civic education in elementary and secondary schools which Kenneth Strike wants strengthened and enriched.[32] However, the knowledge they acquire in such courses does not necessarily influence students' behavior. Recent studies indicate that students' understanding and appreciation of democratic values and processes are strongly influenced by the teaching methods and classroom procedures they encounter in all their courses, and they become interested in political participation as a result of pedagogical strategies that solicit inquiry and invite them to analyze content.[33] Not limited to civics courses, these findings apply across the curriculum.

The findings also confirm hypotheses formulated by progressive educators early in the twentieth century. Once again, political and educational leaders looked with alarm at demographic trends, as great numbers of immigrants entered the country from eastern and southern Europe and from Asia. The search for effective "Americanizing" techniques ranged from adaptations of John Dewey's inquiry pedagogy within a broad variety of content areas to the creation of a formal extra-curriculum. Student-centered but teacher-directed, Dewey's approach viewed learning as active, the consequence of hypothesis-testing by students. They acquired democratic values neither by rote memorization nor recitation but by practicing such values through the unfettered pursuit of knowledge to solve genuine, not merely academic, questions. In Dewey's formulation, the teacher became both the instigator and the exemplary practitioner of inquiry.[34]

The extra-curriculum applied such hypotheses to student experiences beyond classrooms. In the words of one advocate, the extra-curriculum provided the means for "total supervision of the students' social life."[35] Since the school was a society, as Frank Winslow Johnson of the University of Chicago Laboratory School phrased it in 1909, children would be best understood as social beings. Their education occurred through interaction. Schooling was not preparation for life, but life itself. He viewed the school, particularly the high school, as being better equipped than most families or religious institutions for bringing order to student sociability through adult supervision. The "proper preparation" of youth thus utilized all manner of clubs, activities, and athletic events, in addition to the academic curriculum, each "carefully" planned and supervised by teachers. Johnson especially favored student government, "this peculiar method of control," for its practical lessons in citizenship.[36] He cautioned against leaving it without the guidance of teachers, however, for it was "highly artificial" and hence potentially boring to students.

Writing nearly two decades later, Earle Rugg shared Johnson's enthusiasm for the innovation. Student government rendered obsolete such dated approaches to citizenship training as memorizing facts in civics classes.[37] Noting the widespread existence of student government in schools across the country, Rugg expected students to learn citizenship by behaving as citizens in their own (school) society. Student participation in such activities, he argued, was a successful and worthy feature of schooling, an intrinsic good. It also served to maintain discipline, complemented academic goals, promoted school spirit, fostered cooperation among faculty and students, and among the latter inspired respect for law and order. Leonard Koos expanded these claims to encompass extracurricular activities in general because they reinforced the acquisition of civic, social, and moral values.[38] By the time of their Middletown study in the 1920s, the Lynds found a highly organized extra-curriculum, with interscholastic sports at its center, that provided unifying rites and symbols for both schools and the surrounding community.[39] The Lynds' descriptions seemed to assume that readers would recognize the phenomena. In practice, the civics lessons that have been offered to students through transactions with teachers in academic studies and extracurricular activities have reflected contradictory impulses. Against the aim of organizing schools to enable all young people to experience and affirm democratic values stood the realities of direct and indirect exclusion. Direct exclusion targeted specific populations—girls, African Americans, handicapped children, and immigrants. Some were barred from public schools; others were segregated in separate, less accessible, and typically underfunded institutions. Indirect exclusions that watered down content and rewarded intellectual passivity pushed some members of the same populations and still other students to the social margins. These policies and pedagogies suggest why the stated aims of civic education might have been viewed with suspicion by those who were excluded from public schooling opportunities but were nonetheless expected to behave like good citizens.

The exclusionary practices that have undermined the idea of public education and the goals of civic education have admittedly reflected broader social conditions. Given these realities, one might argue that the preparation of citizens cannot be delegated solely to schools. Historically, civic education has resisted being confined to an academic setting because the assignment exceeds the schools' mandates and resources. However effective relative to raising the levels of students' cognitive development, school-based civic education still addresses students who are not protected from social learning. They bring to the classroom lessons acquired in other settings through the pedagogies of experience. Able to see the discrepancies between ideal portrayals of democratic society and their own lives, many behave in school like well-schooled political skeptics.

Over the years, public schools may well have succeeded in delivering instruction on the shared political ideals derived from enlightened pedagogy and the nation's heritage. But there is reason to speculate on the lessons that reached students via the revealed character of the institutions themselves. There was, for example, a problem with the increasing numbers of female teachers. Throughout the nineteenth and early twentieth centuries, they earned lower wages than their male counterparts, were denied full citizenship status in most states, and could not vote in federal elections.[40] Hence, students received civic education from teachers who had limited access to social standing and the office of citizen merely because of their gender. Surviving textbooks, study materials, and teachers' diaries provide information on the sort of instruction in American values and political traditions these women were expected to offer in their classrooms, but one may wonder about the inferences drawn by students—and by the women teachers themselves—from such lessons.

Perhaps the gap between the rhetoric of civic education and the realities of civic life can be bridged by treating the latter explicitly in course content. That is the approach taken by *Civitas: A Framework for Civic Education*, a joint project of the Center for Civic Education and the Council for the Advancement of Citizenship.[41] Arguably the most comprehensive and detailed civics curriculum guide ever made available to teachers, *Civitas* links content and pedagogy for the stated purposes of promoting a common core of knowledge and informed participation in public life. It confronts students with historical and current inequities, invites them to

investigate controversial social issues, and assists teachers in using inquiry as a pedagogical tool. This intentional, systematic, and
scholarly affirmation of educational and democratic values reflects
the influence of R. Freeman Butts, the historian and advocate of
civic education to whom the publication is appropriately dedicated.
Although data on the effectiveness of *Civitas* are still being col-
lected and analyzed, few would question that it establishes a high
academic standard within the civics curriculum literature. Not yet
clear is whether it can undo the often dispiriting civic lessons
American youth still confront through the structures that organize
their social experience.

Uncertain Conclusions

This chapter has focused on episodes in the history of school-based
civic education in the United States. Judged according to the his-
toric purposes of public schools and the nation's democratic principles, the periodic revivals of interest in such programs appear
flawed and ambivalent. If the aims had been restricted to Ameri-
canization strategies, something akin to Horace Mann's inclusionary
rhetoric would have been required to guide school policy and
curriculum. Educational practice, however, has failed to serve even
these pragmatic calculations. Typically, the aims of civic education
have been even more exalted. Again, Horace Mann's formulations
can be used to recall the longstanding insight that the nation
requires citizens whose patriotism is expressed through informed
judgment and political courage. His compromises represented an
early illustration of the persistent gap that has separated civic
education in the United States from its advocates' noble expectations.

Despite the mismatches, contradictions, and ambivalent efforts over the last two centuries, the goals of civic education have
been to seek both good citizens and a good society. These efforts
bring to mind the admonition voiced long ago about the intimate,
causal relation linking individuals in the republic to the common
welfare, and vice versa. Through laws, policies, and myriad daily
interactions, Americans have taught each other how to be citizens.
For good or ill, these lessons still shape the possibility that civic
education can draw the country and its people toward the hope
tacitly and explicitly promised by democratic ideals.

NOTES

1. See, e.g., Horace Mann, "Oration Delivered before the Authorities of the City of Boston, July 4, 1842," *American Journal of Education* 19 (1870): 837–50. (Originally published in Boston, 1842.)

2. B. Edward McClellan, *Schools and the Shaping of Character: Moral Education in America, 1607–Present* (Bloomington, Ind.: ERIC Clearinghouse for Social Studies/Social Science Education and the Social Studies Development Center, Indiana University, 1992), pp. 17–30.

3. Benjamin Rush, "Of the Mode of Education Proper in a Republic," in *The Selected Writings of Benjamin Rush*, Dagobert D. Runes, ed. (New York: Philosophical Library, 1947), p. 92.

4. Donald Warren, *To Enforce Education: A History of the Founding Years of the United States Office of Education* (Detroit: Wayne State University Press, 1974), pp. 27–29.

5. See Noah Webster, "Letter to a Young Gentleman Commencing His Education," in Webster, *A Collection of Papers on Political, Literary, and Moral Subjects* (New York: Webster and Clark, 1843), p. 302.

6. Quoted in James D. Richardson, ed., *A Compilation of the Messages and Papers of the Presidents: 1789–1908* (Washington, D.C.: Bureau of National Literature and Art, 1908), Vol. 1, p. 202.

7. Quoted *ibid.*, p. 409.

8. Elipha White, "Introductory Discourse," American Institute of Instruction, *Lectures and Proceedings* 8 (1837): 3.

9. Kenneth A. Strike, "Foreword," in David C. Bricker, *Classroom Life as Civic Education: Individual Achievement and Student Cooperation in Schools* (New York: Teachers College Press, 1989), p. xv.

10. *Ibid.*

11. See William O. Bourne, *History of the Public School Society of the City of New York* (New York: William Wood, 1870), p. 179.

12. *Connecticut Common School Journal* 1 (May 1839): 113.

13. Superintendent of Common Schools in Connecticut, *Eighth Annual Report* (1853), pp. 180–82.

14. Robert L. McCaul, *The Black Struggle for Public Schooling in Nineteenth-Century Illinois* (Carbondale, Ill.: Southern Illinois University Press, 1987), pp. 8–9.

15. See Jonathan Messerli, *Horace Mann: A Biography* (New York: Alfred A. Knopf, 1972), pp. 246–50.

16. Mann, p. 843.

17. *Ibid.*, p. 837.

18. *Ibid.*, p. 839.

19. *Ibid.*

20. *Ibid.*, p. 841.

21. Warren, p. 29.

22. See Vincent P. Lannie, ed., *Henry Barnard: American Educator* (New York: Teachers College Press, 1974); and Warren, pp. 105–106.

23. Henry Steele Commager, "Schoolmaster to America," in *Noah Webster's American Spelling Book* (New York: Bureau of Publications, Teachers College, Columbia University, 1962), pp. 1–2.

24. McCaul, pp. 4–7.

25. Mann, p. 841.

26. Bessie L. Pierce, *Civic Attitudes in American School Textbooks* (Chicago: University of Chicago Press, 1930), pp. 121–25.

27. Messerli, p. 346.

28. See John Dewey, *Interest and Effort in Education* (Carbondale, Ill.: Southern Illinois University Press, 1975), pp. 7–11. (Originally published by Houghton Mifflin in 1913.)

29. Bricker, p. 97.

30. See Judith V. Torney, A.N. Oppenheim, and Russell F. Farnen, *Civic Education in Ten Countries: An Empirical Study* (New York: John Wiley and Sons, 1975).

31. See William B. Fetters, George H. Brown, and Jeffrey A. Owings, *High School Seniors: A Comparative Study of the Classes of 1972 and 1980* (Washington, D.C.: Government Printing Office, 1984); and Arthur Levine, *When Dreams and Heroes Died: A Portrait of Today's College Student* (San Francisco: Jossey-Bass, 1980).

32. Bricker, p. xv; also, Howard E. Wilson, *Education for Citizenship: Report of the Regents' Inquiry* (New York: McGraw-Hill, 1938).

33. Judith Torney-Purta, "Psychological Perspectives on Enhancing Civic Education Through the Education of Teachers," *Journal of Teacher Education* 34, no. 6 (November–December 1983): 30–34.

34. Dewey, pp. 95–96.

35. Frank Winslow Johnson, "The Social Organization of the High School," *School Review* 17 (December 1909): 679.

36. *Ibid.*, 668.

37. Earle Rugg, "Special Types of Activities: Student Participation in Student Government," in *Extra-Curricular Activities*, Twenty-fifth Yearbook of the National Society for the Study of Education, Part II, Guy M. Whipple, ed. (Bloomington, Ill.; Public School Publishing Co., 1926), pp. 127–40.

38. Leonard V. Koos, "Analysis of the General Literature on Extra-Curricular Activities," *Ibid.*, pp. 1–22.

39. Robert S. Lynd and Helen Merrell Lynd, *Middletown: A Study in American Culture* (New York: Harcourt, Brace and Co., 1929), pp. 211–22.

40. See Susan B. Carter, "Incentives and Rewards to Teaching," in Donald Warren, ed., *American Teachers: Histories of a Profession at Work* (New York: Macmillan, 1989), pp. 49–62.

41. *Civitas: A Framework for Civic Education* (Calabasas, Cal.: Center for Civic Education, 1991).

Chapter 8

✧

Preparing Citizens for a Decent Society: Educating for Virtue

Introduction

This chapter is based on certain presuppositions about the nature and purpose of education within our society which it would be well to make clear at the beginning. It is not my purpose here to defend these presuppositions, though they are defensible. Rather, having made them clear, I will attempt to understand their implications for the proper role of schools in initiating children into citizenship.

The three presuppositions of my argument are: (1) citizenship in a democratic republic is an office; (2) morality is a social construct, not a discoverable ontological entity; and (3) a person is required to possess certain virtues in order to hold the office of citizen; not just anyone will do.

In our society we are not merely subjects; we are citizens. This is true, but often not considered in discussion about schools and society. What does it mean to say we are citizens? The simplest way to answer is to point to the fact that we are not merely inhabitants of this country, passively subject to its laws and/or rulers. While we are properly subject to the laws of the country, duly made, citizenship is more than this; it is, at least potentially, active.

At least in theory, as citizens we are involved in our own government, specifically through our representatives. That is, we select our representatives through the ballot, and can influence the laws that govern us by whom we select to make them. We can also organize into lobbying groups to secure legislation that concerns us. Further, many states, though not the national government, allow for initiative, referendum, or recall, providing more direct participation on the part of citizens.

Thus, while we are expected as citizens to obey the laws of the land, that is not the end of the expectations of citizens. We are also expected to take an active role in framing those laws. It is not farfetched to suggest that to be a citizen in a democratic republic such as the United States is to hold an office. So, this chapter will consider what it means to recognize that citizenship is an office, not just an accident of residence. Citizens have a function beyond mere obedience and support.

Second, we need to consider the notion that morality is a social construct, not an empirically discoverable entity. This is not to say that morality is not real; it is. But its reality, as Durkheim instructed us, is social, and not discoverable outside a social context.[1]

We need to separate this realization from the moral relativism with which it is often confused. Two points should be considered in this regard: (1) while there may not be any one best moral code or system (and the presumption is that there is not), it does not follow from this that some moral codes are not better than others, and (2) it does not follow from the fact that there are no proofs of superiority that there are therefore no justifiable standards by which to compare one moral code to another. So the fact that moral codes are socially constructed and fitted to the society that constructs them in no way entails that all moral codes and societies are equally good or defensible. Nevertheless, it does tell us that justifiable moral codes are not in the world to be discovered; they are human inventions.

Third, not just anyone is suited to be a citizen, since the office, as with any other office, places certain demands on the officeholder. This proposition, taken literally, presents us with a paradox, since by definition all members of American society are in fact citizens. And so we should modify the claim: not just anyone can be a good and worthy citizen. Certain virtues are required of citizens, just as of any officeholder.

This latter claim should be uncontroversial. Every society needs certain virtues from its citizens: virtue is, in one sense, merely the ability to live socially with others, meeting their legitimate expectations. Hence, even societies which we would judge to be fundamentally corrupt, such as Stalin's Soviet Union or Hitler's Germany, needed their citizens to have certain virtues, such as courage, loyalty, and fidelity. However, we are not concerned here with the needs of a corrupt society; we want to know what it means to construct and maintain what we can judge to be a decent society. First of all, we need to attend to the meaning of that phrase: "a decent society."

A Decent Society

To begin, then, does it make sense even to talk about a decent society? I will argue that it does. It is most clearly the case in the negative; there are societies that are clearly indecent in their treatment of their own citizens, and which we have good reason to judge as not decent societies. Examples of these might include Hitler's Germany, Stalin's Soviet Union, South Africa under the regime of apartheid, and the People's Republic of China while it represses dissent. By looking at societies that are clearly not decent, we can begin to define decency in at least negative space. Taking as the minimum criterion the requirement that decent societies do not cause harm to their own citizens, each of the above societies fails this fundamental test.

This brings us immediately to a central thesis of this chapter: moral judgments about the practices of other societies, and about practices of our own as well, are possible, necessary, and justifiable. While we can never know with certainty that the judgment we make is correct, that need not—and should not—deter us from making such judgments.[2] Further, Thomas Kuhn, among others, makes a persuasive argument that there is no such thing as certain knowledge, even in science, where it was once thought to be possible. Scientific knowledge is, according to Kuhn's view, the best possible reasoned judgments about the nature of the world, based on socially contingent screens he calls "paradigms," which order our perceptions of the world for us.[3] Nonetheless, we launch astronauts into space and bring them back, launch probes to the edge of the solar system, and develop cancer treatments which greatly extend human life. The point is that we act and make judgments in the natural world without the certainty that we seem to demand in the moral world, and without which we claim we are unable to act. Kuhn makes clear that making judgments on the best possible evidence, as defined by our socially negotiated interpretations of reality, is not the same as relativism.

So, the claim is not that there are objective criteria upon which we can *know* that these societies are not decent, but rather that we have good reason to make a *judgment* about their decency, and that we have good reason to find them lacking. This is not the same as knowing that 2 + 2 = 4, but most of our knowledge is not of this definitional type. It is a judgment, not a mere whimsical preference. Preferring to live in the Sweden of today rather than in the Germany of 1935 is not at all like preferring chocolate ice cream to vanilla. What we are doing in the former case is making a *moral* judgment about the Nazi system's moral inferiority to the Swedish one.[4]

There is an intuitive sense to the term "a decent society." The meaning can be explored at length, though that is not our purpose here. For now, I wish to note two propositions that are posited more than defended here: (1) it does make sense to judge a society's decency, both absolutely and relative to other societies; and (2) we can analyze a society's decency in either a minimal or maximal sense. A minimally decent society does not do unnecessary harm to its own members, or to others with whom it comes in contact. The maximal sense of decency is more difficult to summarize, but it requires that there be agreements about, among other things, definitions of what constitutes "harm." It is possible that the difference between the minimal decency and a maximal one is the inclusiveness of who is protected from "harm" and how the term is defined. These are issues for another essay; the point here is simply that it makes sense to talk about social decency. There are standards of judgment that can be explicated and defended.

Social and Individual Decency

What is the relationship between a decent society and decent individuals? Once we remember the proposition that morality is a social construct, the answer becomes obvious: a decent society will be one with decent citizens. In fact, the proposition comes close to being definitional: a society provides the standards of morality to which its members become normed. Raised in a society with pervasively decent standards, individuals will be much more likely to become decent than otherwise. Further, it hardly makes sense to say a society is decent but its members, by and large, are not.

Of course, decency here is without content; the analysis holds whether the standards are those of minimal decency, which may not actually amount to recognizable decency, or maximal decency. Whatever standard is taken as the measure of societal decency, it seems that the members of that society must instantiate those standards (by and large and on the whole). And this is where we can begin to consider the role that education will and must play in the (re?)creation of a decent society.

Virtue and Decency

We will continue this analysis using the assumption of minimal decency. We have seen the inadequacy of this standard, but the point of continuing with it is that, even by this inadequate standard, virtue is necessary for decency to exist in a society. We can assume that any fuller standard than that of non-harm will rely even more strongly on a robust set of civic virtues.

Any society requires certain virtuous actions from its citizens. This is phrased so as not to claim that the citizens must actually be virtuous, since that is not necessarily the case; society might be served by citizens without virtue who act virtuously. Dogs do not lie, but that is not because they are honest. Individuals of murderous intent, kept under sufficient surveillance, do not murder, but not out of regard for their fellow citizens. Would-be thieves do not steal from well-guarded banks, but not because they are law-abiding. The point is Aristotle's, that there is a difference between virtuous acts, and virtuous acts done virtuously.[5] There can be many reasons why people act in accordance with the moral norms of their society, but in any society with pretensions to democratic tendencies, it is considered better if virtuous acts are done virtuously rather than otherwise. This is because a fundamental premise of a democratic society is that individuals should be self-governing. But this is not possible when individuals act in ways that offend the moral code of the society. For a society to be decent its citizens must, on the whole and by and large, act decently. But, by our standards, a decent society is also one that places minimum restraints on its citizens' actions. A police officer on every corner may make cities safer places to live, but, by the standards of a liberal democracy, police officers on every corner cannot make cities more decent. Therefore, education, both in and outside school, must encourage children to become the sort of citizens who live decently without being forced to do so.

If children are to live in society, it is to their own benefit that their education be such that they become normed to the standards of decency of their society, since they will be required to live by those standards. This raises, of course, the problem of social decency. We may be norming children to standards that are not even minimally decent, in ways we cannot even perceive. In truth, there seems to be no alternative to making a good-faith effort to evaluate these standards in the light of the best moral reasoning of which we are capable.

As one of the social institutions responsible for helping children attain full membership in society, schools must play their part in the encouragement of virtue.[6] There are two categories of virtues we will briefly consider: civic virtues and educational virtues.[7]

Citizenship and Virtue

To restate part of the argument as it relates to citizenship and virtue, even morally bankrupt societies require virtue of their citizens or subjects. But this requirement is both stronger and broader in any society where citizens are supposed to be self-governing. This is so because if the citizens of such a state are not virtuous, either they will act in ways that violate the principles of decency, or the state will act in ways that violate the principles of self-governance. In either case, a liberal democracy that aspires to social decency must either encourage personal decency in its citizens or betray the liberal democratic premises that give it its legitimacy.

A Brief Case Study

Without going into the intricacies of the matter, it is instructive to look briefly at the controversy currently surrounding the move for "political correctness" in the light of the preceding discussion. Such a look may help us to understand better what is at stake in that issue, as well as in the broader consideration of what makes a decent society. We will briefly visit the attempts to limit offensive speech on many college campuses.

The issue of offensive speech is usually cast as an attempt to prohibit the public use of certain racial, sexist, or homophobic epithets. This is an example of what was considered above in the claim that a liberal democracy does not require that citizens be virtuous, so long as they act virtuously. These efforts to prevent offensive speech in no way purport to lessen racism. It is considered sufficient to prevent racist action through threat of official sanction. Depending on one's point of view, this prohibition is either an admirable attempt to make society more civil by preventing verbal attacks on some groups, or an invocation of noble motives to support an ill-considered suspension of the First Amendment.

This chapter will remain agnostic on this aspect of the debate, while pointing to some of its broader implications in the context of social decency and liberal democracy.

First of all, some premises: (1) by the generally espoused standards of the society, decent people do not attack others, verbally or otherwise, for their race, gender, or sexual orientation; (2) free speech is a core value of any democratic society; and (3) at some point in a society where there are frequent and flagrant violations of the prevailing standards of decency, either the standards will be re-evaluated and changed, or they will be upheld by coercive measures. I believe we currently stand at this point in the matter of offensive speech; those in positions of power, in universities especially, are being asked to use their power to prevent such public speech. Given the two alternatives outlined in premise 3 above, failure to prevent offensive speech, and its continuation, may lead to a reconsideration of the proposition that decent people do not do such things. For example, "After all, Charlie is a pretty nice guy, all-in-all. If he uses racist epithets, maybe that's not such a bad thing to do."

So, we have good reason to want to prevent the common acceptance of such speech. The question becomes one of means and ends. We may have come to this pass because we have taken too literally the moral neutrality which is part of our liberal tradition. In a social system that denies the use of moral claims in educating children, we give up the most powerful means we have at our disposal for shaping the character of our citizens. We can no longer explain to children we hear using such language that it is "wrong" to do so, since we have abandoned the concept of "wrong." We are thus left with two options: acceptance of the unacceptable or legal sanctions against it. The whole point of this argument is that it is better, for both the individual and society, to educate so that we encourage the existence of virtue, even if that entails some limitations on the free development of each individual.

Part of the job of education, as a social enterprise, is to contribute to the quality of our society. The failure to shape children's character in socially desirable ways entails a later choice by society between coercively imposing compliance on them or tolerating the intolerable with its potential for unravelling the social fabric. And from the individual's point of view, it may be worth considering that, if children are to live in a society where open expressions of racism bring condemnation, they are likely to be happier individuals if their characters are so shaped by education that they are not in fact racists.

Virtue

The notion of virtue used here essentially follows Pincoffs' notion: virtue is an attribute that makes it reasonable for others to admire that aspect of us.[8] It is the Aristotelian ability to do the right thing at the right time in the right way for the right reasons.

It is in this sense also that Galston frames his consideration of what he calls "Civic Virtues." Briefly, and without endorsing the specific list of virtues he holds up to us as necessary for a liberal democracy to exist, I would endorse his insight that there are in fact some virtues which are necessary for a liberal democracy to function. This becomes clearer if we also keep in mind the earlier observation that citizenship is the holding of an office, and that this office, like any other, places demands on the officeholder.

Further, Pritchard makes clear that education is impossible without some virtues. Following MacIntyre,[9] Pritchard unpacks the notion that education is a practice, and that every practice has virtues internal to itself. Again, without endorsing the specific list of virtues Pritchard presents, we can see the force of his argument clearly: virtues are those qualities of character that allow us to engage in certain endeavors successfully, or at least well.[10] Pritchard convincingly makes the case that unless children develop certain virtues, they cannot be truly educated. The exercise of those virtues is simply part of what it means to be engaged in education.

If this is true for education, it seems inescapably true for citizenship. If we are to be good citizens of a liberal democracy we must possess certain virtues or be forced to act as though we had them. The same is true, of course, for any form of social organization, although the specific virtues or their form of expression change. If we decide not to be a liberal democracy any more, abandoning the tensions and conflicts in favor of some other form of government, we will still need certain virtues; the list might just be different.

Education, Citizenship, and Virtue

To recapitulate, there are two distinct, but interrelated questions: how to help children enter society, and how to keep in mind the question of the decency of the society. There seems no reason to question that schools have a role to play in each of these tasks.

Given the fact that society funds schools for the purpose of educating its young, it would be peculiar if preparation for membership in that society were not a legitimate expectation. Further, given the nature of our society, membership is citizenship, and so the preparation that schools provide must include training for the office of citizen.

What might this mean? In the first place, that an individual's freedom is a means, not an end. That is, freedom is not valued for its own sake, but for the role it allows the citizen to play in the construction of a decent society.[11] We do not value the freedom to become a monster. We should care that our children do not feel free to emulate Hitler, or the Los Angeles police who so brutally beat Rodney King. One of the things we want to teach children is how to ask questions, but included in that teaching must be a sense of what counts as standards for good questions and for good answers. The idea that we should "let each become all that s/he is capable of becoming" should give us a moment of sober reflection; we must never forget that human potential is the power to destroy as well as create. We are as capable of evil as of good. Education exists to limit this freedom, and to direct it toward good ends. Among other things, humans possess the potential to become moral monsters. We should try to discourage the realization of that potential, even if that necessitates what might be seen as limitations of free expression of the self.

Which ends are good? Here, too, the school can play a role. Two roles, in fact. First, it can be the forum in which the community can ask this question of itself: "What are the standards of decency and goodness we wish to pass on to future generations?" Currently, the local schools are as close as this society comes to the Greek marketplace, where people can come together to debate issues that concern them. Because of their concern for their children, parents and community members are often willing to participate in discussions about textbook selection and course content. Indeed, these discussions often take place at the insistence of the community. Sometimes these discussions generate more heat than light, coming as they do after the school has offended some group of parents who then confront the school with an organized protest. But the local school may as well serve as a place for reasoned and principled discussion, extended over time, about the sort of people we want to encourage our children to become. Second, schools can become one means through which those standards judged by the adults to be worthy are examined, applied, discussed, and passed on to the children.

These standards will inevitably be flawed, and this a concern. For if we take the moral mission of schools seriously, we are then at risk of passing on flawed, even corrupt or evil, moral standards to our children, and doing so effectively. This is a danger, but it is not clear exactly what its implications are, or how to avoid it. Surely, we are not in a better situation if we do no moral teaching at all. Empirically, it seems to me to be the case (the more clearly the older I and my children get) that children do not simply accept at face value the teachings of the older generation. Moral standards are accepted with modifications and with due notation of inconsistencies and hypocrisies. What we *can* give children is a clear sense of the existence and importance of the moral domain. Further, we can give children a sense of what it means to take moral standards seriously in making decisions, and what it looks like to do moral reasoning. Of course, it goes without saying—or, more precisely, it should go without saying but does not—that this can only be done by teachers who take their own moral responsibilities seriously, and are willing to model what a morally-lived life looks like, what moral reasoning is, and to involve their students, in ways appropriate to their development, in such reasoning.

Conclusion

This chapter is not intended to solve the problems it raises. Its purpose is more modest: to suggest a way to see those problems that might help us solve them. Certainly, no clear picture of decency is put forth here. However, there is such a thing as decency, and we do need to take its nature seriously. We need to do so, however, in a public forum where differing voices are heard, but where a consensual voice can be striven for on certain matters central to a decent society. We need to be united by more than our differences. The schools might just serve as that public forum. Parents can be involved in public discussion about what their children ought to be taught; children can be included in a conversation in the schools about decency and moral reasoning.

There are risks in this approach; social consensus might be oppressive, narrow, and socially destructive. But not to have a vision of a decent society to put forth for examination in a public forum, and to encourage our children to take part in, seems nihilistic and far more dangerous.

NOTES

1. See Emile Durkheim, *On Moral Education: A Study in the Theory and Application of the Sociology of Education* (New York: The Free Press, 1961), Chapter One.

2. In preparing the original version of this chapter for presentation as part of an AERA symposium, I and my colleagues had ample opportunity for critical comment on each others' papers. By this point in mine, someone had usually inscribed, "John, who is 'us'?", or some variant thereof. I must confess I do not know exactly, though I have a hunch, as Joan Burstyn also suggests in her contribution to this discussion, that the search for an identifiable "us" is an urgent agenda item for American society.

3. Thomas Kuhn, *The Structure of Scientific Revolutions*, 2nd ed. (Chicago: University of Chicago Press, 1970).

4. There has been a shift in language here. I began talking about "decency," and am now talking about "morality." The change, it seems to me, is not only a natural one, but is unavoidable. What we are talking about with this notion of decency is indeed a moral judgment—it is moral decency with which we are concerned.

5. Aristotle, *Nichomachean Ethics.* Translated by Terence Irwin. (Indianapolis: Hacket, 1985), pp. 39–40 (lines 1105a17–1105b12).

6. I owe this concept of "encouraging" virtue to a paper by Ivor Pritchard that seems to me to capture the sense of what we should be doing: it is less than indoctrination or inculcation, but more than taking

a hands-off approach to the formation of children's character. (See Ivor Pritchard, "Education Without Virtue," presented at the annual meeting of the American Educational Research Association, Chicago, Ill., 1991.)

7. For educational virtues, see *Ibid;* for civic virtues, see William Galston, "Civic Education in the Liberal State," In *Liberalism and the Moral Life*, Nancy L. Rosenblum, (ed.), (Cambridge: Harvard University Press, 1989), pp. 89–101.

8. See Edmund L. Pincoffs, *Quandaries and Virtues: Against Reductivism in Ethics* (Lawrence, Kansas: University Press of Kansas, 1986).

9. See Alasdair MacIntyre, *After Virtue* (Notre Dame: University of Notre Dame Press, 1984).

10. This is not to say that the activity itself is a worthwhile activity. We may, for example, condemn war but admire the courage and dedication it engenders (which would explain why William James would wish to discover a moral equivalent); we might find the brutality of boxing appalling, and still appreciate the force of will and physical conditioning that boxers exhibit.

11. One might wish to contest this proposition. If one does so, one invariably must do so from the point of view of the individual, not of the society; such an argument can only get going by forgetting that education is a social (and socially funded) activity, and that schools are social institutions.

Mary B. Stanley

Chapter 9

✧

Service Learning as Civic Education: Difference, Culture War, and the Material Basis of a Good Life

Introduction

Recent concerns with diversity, the so-called culture wars, and the waning consensus on the definition of the good life or scarcity regarding its material prerequisites should agreement be reached on its substance, have led some educators to explore the civic possibilities of service learning.[1] Service learning as presently understood in the field includes two essential aspects: 1) that service be provided to persons or communities in need, with efforts made to have communities define the nature of the need; and 2) that reflection attend the service experience. Increasingly, such reflection is viewed as best accomplished within an academic setting, usually through courses that require a service component. The definition of service learning in the National and Community Service Trust Act of 1993 is probably as good a summary as any of what service learning, to mainstream advocates, entails:

> Service Learning means a method under which students or participants learn and develop through active participation in thoughtfully organized service that: is conducted in and meets the needs of a community and is coordinated with an elementary, secondary, institution of higher education, or community service program, and with the community; helps foster civic responsibility; is integrated into and enhances the academic curriculum of the students or the educational components of the community service program in which the participants enroll; and includes structured time for the students and participants to reflect on the service experience.

As a practitioner of service learning in higher education, I believe that service learning, regardless of Congressional intent, has at its core the re-discovery of society through action. In that discovery, students and their teachers engage the question of what is a valuable society in the context of society as presently constituted. I would agree with David Thorton Moore of New York University, who argues that the reflection that accompanies service learning will invariably become *critical* reflection, regardless of the intentions of its practitioners and supporters. Moore argues that service learning generates fruitful tensions which can best, perhaps only, be explored through critical discourse. He grounds his claims in critical theory, the general orientation called post-structuralism, and the work of Habermas, Derrida, and Foucault.

To Moore, service learning "arrives at an image of meaning as situated and fragile; of knowledge as negotiated and interactional; and learning as dialectic and active."[2]

I will take up Moore's concern with language, discourse, and meaning later in this chapter. For now, it is enough to state that through service learning young people are guided into civil society. The literature on civil society is vast and growing, and includes long-standing controversies regarding what is meant by civil society or even whether, given the modern and postmodern condition, it can exist.[3] Whatever its definition, with the fall of communism in the former Soviet empire, academics, political leaders, and ordinary citizens throughout the world have witnessed the disassociation of a civil society from a political regime. The drama of that possibility is a warning to any political community. A political regime once viewed as impregnable has undergone the ultimate delegitimation, in part due to the experiences and dissatisfactions of ordinary people fed up with daily life as ordered and limited by the regime. Metaphors regarding the rending of the social fabric and its political consequences have taken on a concrete intensity with the collapse of the Soviet system. It is a warning no political community can ignore.

Service learning "situates" students in our civil society. Once there, students are invited to grasp, criticize, or reaffirm the abstract political values that legitimate our polity and may or may not be enacted in the day-to-day experience of persons and communities. Without such experience and critical reflection upon it, some educators fear that young people may be led into one or another of the twin dangers that undermine a democratic regime: hopeless and bitter cynicism, or abstract ideological celebration which easily accommodates itself to human suffering. In contrast, service learning offers young people the opportunity to engage the world as actor and knower in a manner that affirms the hope that our society, if found wanting as a context for nurturing democratic values and human dignity, can be reformed. At minimum, service learning enrolls students in the moral dramaturgy of bearing witness to human suffering, an action that suggests we are a compassionate, if not always just, polity.

Through service learning, young people (I will discuss college-aged young people, though the K–12 service learning movement is gathering increasing steam) confront society at the micro level of individuals, the communal level of cultural groups or "communities," and/or, perhaps most challenging, at the macro level of institutions and social structure. Commitments to service learning often focus on helping students explore only one of these three levels of social life. Ideological orientation may dispose an educator or an institution of higher education to organize service, and increasingly service learning, in ways that reinforce a particular view of the polity, civil society, and of citizenship, emphasizing on the one hand micro freedoms or on the other macro determinisms.

For example, it is not surprising that William F. Buckley embraces a language of service infused with the notion of individualism, gratitude, and privilege.[4] Individuals with much or even not so much (Buckley encourages the modestly privileged, also, to appreciate their blessings) are grateful and give of themselves to individuals with little or less. The language of those who adopt such a perspective remains dense with assumptions regarding the morally redemptive benefits of service, at least to those who prove they are worthy of their privileges through their acts of generosity and kindness.

Though young people may become sober and humble in their appreciation for what has been given them, they are unlikely to inquire too deeply into the origins of privilege or of want. Nor are they encouraged to press for fundamental social change, since such change may eliminate many fruitful opportunities to create an individual moral self through service to "the underprivileged," or "needy." The poor, ill, and old indeed are always with us and more thanks to them! In this context, a valuable society may be one that flourishes on inequality of condition, the neediness of some and the generosity of others generating powerful social bonds. The social fabric is woven together by innumerable acts of micro decency. The civic education requisite to this vision of a good society demands service. The learning that attends service would have at its core the complex literature of charity and philanthropy, and many hortatory calls to the virtues of self-denial and discipline. Any questioning of the nature of the needs addressed through service, that is, whether they result from social processes open to human intervention or are "natural," and humanly unavoidable, is unlikely to be on the learning agenda.

If, on the right, the origin and maintenance of privilege and need through the structure of society is the great secret to be avoided in the learning attending service learning, on the left, the mystery to be gently passed over is the complicity of persons in their fate; persons who may appear to themselves not as victims of social structures but as autonomous adults who screwed up and need help, or even children who do need as much individual assistance as possible to spin them away from the bad choices they might well make. To those of the traditional left, service learning is compromised from the beginning if it does not have at its center issues of equality, social justice, and false consciousness (in its various forms, e.g., resistance of people to the knowledge of their own victimhood). To those of the traditional left, students must evaluate whether the standards of equality and justice used in rhetoric have been enacted in practice. Outcomes of such an assessment must be interpreted by macro theories regarding how structure and ideology operate in micro social interactions. Service learning without such a dimension is mere propaganda and ritual, not education fit for democratic citizens.

Is there, then, any ideologically neutral approach to the learning that attends service? Is there a service learning not about preparing citizens for some version of a valuable society? Is service learning fundamentally civic learning because it is about the discovery of political values in use and the preparation of citizens for life in a particular civil society ordered by a particular political regime? Is there a difference between civic education and political education? To use Aristotle's distinction, is the learning in service learning essentially practical, leading to wise political judgment? Or, on the contrary, can it be solely theoretical, leading to a complex, fulsome, and, in some sense, true knowledge of society and its processes? More fundamentally still, are such distinctions between practice and theory, so critical to Western political thinking, now irrelevant in the new American polity emerging out of the transformations within civil society, a society which may itself be resistant to domestication by abstract theory that seems no longer relevant to experience in the late twentieth century? Or is service learning the implicit means to test new theoretical models of society—global, virtual, multi-cultural, post-structural, postmodern—against the lived experiences of actual persons and communities?

In order to explore these questions, I will return to the three challenges introduced at the beginning of this chapter: diversity, cultural war, and the material basis and definition of a good life.

Needless to say, the three are related. Cultural war is about competing definitions of what a good life is, or even whether the concept of a good life is itself tainted by its association with Western political theory. Further, demands for diversity may trigger the fear that once a wide range of visions regarding the use of collective resources and how to order collective life enter political space, profound gridlock or chaos results. Looming above all such considerations may be the apprehension that our polity does not command the material resources necessary to support diverse and competing visions of a good life, a valuable society, or valued persons.

I will examine how service learning as presently conceived and practiced addresses each of these three challenges as it continues its agenda of helping—intentionally or not—young people discover the tension between rhetoric regarding a valued society and valued persons and the actual practices of people, communities, and institutions. I will tease out the civically educative dimension of service learning in reference to these three challenges.

Diversity

Post-World War II assumptions regarding what everyone really wants have been seriously eroded. The good life as posited by the traditional left and right has fallen on hard times. The left's materialism, commitment to labor as collective and humanizing, notions of equality and solidarity, and analysis of late capitalism do not seem to capture the allegiance of those seemingly most in need of the attending praxis. The prudence, tolerance, and neutrality of the moderate left, as represented by classical liberals, seems to advance too thin a definition of a good life, given the intense battles over what sort of lives people should be given the moral space to lead.

On the libertarian right, irony abounds regarding who might authentically view herself an entrepreneur and a social Darwinist, given her actual vulnerabilities to the churn of late capitalism. The good life as posited by the libertarian right has so drifted from its moorings in the attainable that young people narrate their expectations as premised upon declining opportunity, regardless of their affinity for Rush Limbaugh. On the conservative right, totalizing visions of a return to one Christian (or Muslim or Jewish or . . .), absolutist civil society supported by a sympathetic political regime unafraid to affirm one version of a valuable society chills anxious moderates of both our main political parties.

Whether or not in reaction to the collapse of the right/left Western hegemony regarding visions of lives worth living, alternative good lives are sprouting everywhere. The materialism that fueled capitalism, communism, and socialism has lost its grip as social class has lost its dominant explanatory power.[5] Although classism, sexism, and racism are supposedly equal in their contributions to human woe, post-colonial ideologies of resistance and affirmation throughout the world and in advanced industrial societies, in their celebration of the suppressed cultures of former colonial peoples or women or gays, do not focus on class. Minorities of all sorts are invited to consider their history as a sequence of hegemony and noble resistance, victimhood and eventual triumph, colonized selves and reclaimed selves. Even the Christian right has adopted the stance of persecuted minority, the truth of whose message is suppressed by powerful, godless institutions.

In a profound sense, the focal issue is the self as embedded in cultures. While mainstream elites may puzzle over or denigrate "identity politics," viewing the rituals of membership and defense of group particularity as mere status politics, many citizens are impassioned by the challenge of identity at a time when taken-for-granted principles are challenged in the academy and in the street. The ordering constructs of Western, colonial patriarchy appear under siege; maps and mines, commodities and missionaries, technology and profit, central planning and market forces, epistemology and literature, grand narratives and calendars. Or, on the other hand, these constructs are embraced with such tenacity as to appear atavistic and dangerous. This assault and reaction is heady stuff. It is certainly not about bread alone.

What possible type of civic education can accommodate itself to a polity or world order constituted by no geographical boundaries (gender and sexual orientation), or fraught with contested homelands (former colonial peoples, African Americans, immigrants, and refugees of all sorts), or carried on outside the realm of material reality (spiritual claims challenging Western understanding of reality)? Or to polities and peoples that reassert existing boundaries, commitments to homelands, or claims about reality in their most rigid, fundamentalist forms? Perhaps a civic education ordered around the concept of diversity, which gives extraordinary importance to the function and exploration of language and culture.[6] Indeed, several authors in this collection, and, as noted above, in the service learning literature, have selected language as their site for examining the reformist, even revolutionary, possibilities of civic education, identifying language as the carrier of unacknowledged assumptions about the way society ought to be ordered and in whose interests.

Citizenship education in the American tradition has been until quite recently a homogenizing force at the level of language and culture. True, advocates of civic education have always recognized that in some fashion the United States is and always has been a nation of immigrants. Periodically, social critics have argued that cultural differences might be the source of an enlivened democratic community; its dynamism because of pluralism.[7]

However, most frequently the underlying assumption regarding immigration, at least to non-nativists, has been that though immigrants were initially culturally different, the act of immigration suggested motives and capacities in them that reflected universal American virtues, e.g., love of freedom, ambition, and individualism. Further, identity as citizen included a well-known capacity for free political speech and for the internal dialogue of conscience. Those of an environmentalist orientation have long held that the very experience of interacting with nature and each other in American free space was conducive to the nurturance of both. Nativists and racists, often using innate limitations as their explanation, are of course skeptical regarding whether immigrants or those of particular races did and do have the capacities for achieving the prerequisites for membership in a democratic society.

Past and present social and political critics and my fellow contributors to this volume have also been skeptical regarding the range of such *free* speech for *most* Americans, immigrants or not. To them, the resulting conscience is not free to choose much at all, since consciousness is—to them—the meta-language of unexamined assumptions that support capitalism.

More recent critiques of language despair of ever ridding ourselves of the oppressive, colonizing structures that slip into our minds with our very first words. Perhaps in reaction, others cling to the word so closely as to reduce the complexity of multiple narratives to the literalism of fundamentalist beliefs.

Complex as theories of language and freedom have become, many groups and their members simply do the best they can to reclaim and rename the social world beginning with the self. To those whose language reflects a consensus on a reality now increasingly under attack, the dizzying effort to open up speech to the claims of those with no interest in Western standards of evidence, and its attendant logical constraints upon public discourse, appears frightening.

How does service learning provide young people with the ability to navigate such a fluid social world, where standards of evidence and even reality appear contested? Where language is often not a bridge but a barrier? And toward what ends should young people direct their service?

The service learning literature of the last ten years is brimming with reminders that service confronts students with unavoidable diversity. If not all service learning advocates embrace the seemingly arcane theorists of postmodernism or sociolinguistics, they are aware that through service young people encounter multiple social worlds. The mastery of diversity is promoted among advocates as a critical civic skill, to be practiced in the context of service learning. Indeed, one root of service learning is international programs which have long invited college-aged students to immerse themselves fully in cultural differences, among Western, European cultures. The more recent service learning literature invites students to recognize the complex diversity of American society, often right outside the door and down the hill, or to consider Africa, Asia, or Latin America as the only true opportunities for deep cultural immersion.

The recognition that American civil society is diverse but that its political culture had its origins in a presumably more homogeneous social order is not new. Late nineteenth- and early twentieth-century civic pedagogy was specifically directed at the challenge of diversity. R. Freeman Butts recounts that history for us,[8] and we are reminded by historian Richard Hofstadter that defeating an "immigrant politics" was then the object of intense mobilization among nativist reformers.[9] We even had a counterpoint in the settlement house movement, a service learning commitment if there ever was one. However, in retrospect, the humane effort to celebrate immigrant culture, led by such women as Jane Addams, Grace Abbott, Sophonisba Breckinridge, and Julia Lathrop, and even Addams's profound recognition of the modern demands democracy and equality make on a society ordered by concentrated wealth and exploited labor, appear inadequate to address diversity in the 1990s.[10] However, what is still compelling about the work and thought of these women is their awareness, perhaps because they were women, that social reform was about immersion in civil society. Such reform had to address not abstract notions of justice and honor but the quotidian concerns of mothers and fathers, children and workers, consumers and immigrants.

The young woman invited into public life by Jane Addams and her colleagues in the 1890s was reminded that she must stand with her neighbors, no matter how strange their dress and odd their habits, mediate their concerns, and be the catalyst for creating a new organic city, perhaps nation. The reformers' strategy would be the nurturance of neither charity nor even organized philanthropy. It was to be the gathering of data and facts in their roles as compassionate witnesses, good neighbors, and initiators of new forms of social interaction. Their goals did move from civil society into political action. For all their attention to the matrix of social life, they sought sound legislation addressing injustices made clear, logical and compelling.[11]

In the 1990s, injustices are not so clear, their causes and solutions are opaque, and the moral imperative to address them is not uniformly compelling. Students in service discover that left/right distinctions, the dramatic class-based analysis which has served social critics well since our own revolution, cannot so easily contextualize their experience nor give coherence to their action. Solidarity forever seems an increasingly elusive goal, and social class analysis is seemingly inadequate to produce it. Gender, race, sexual orientation, cultures of all sorts generate competing frameworks. There is no one simple way to do good. This at the very time when advanced social and humane theory invites students to be skeptical of all frameworks. Sometimes experience invites students to use the aging tools of Western analysis; sometimes experience demands students jettison those tools altogether. Sometimes faculty hope students find in experience the utility of beloved theories; sometimes faculty hope students discover the meagerness of theory, given the chaos, drama, and intensity of feeling enacted in people's lives.

Here is the challenge for the educator: how to simultaneously order and contextualize experience while recognizing that for many academics, listeners of radio talk shows, and puzzled young people there is not only diversity, but some would argue, a cultural war being fought in the streets and alleys of everyday life. This war is fought not so that all can become Americans, finally entering one admirable and compelling story, but over what the American experience has been and will be and whether we will ever agree upon what to say about the past, hope for the future, and do in the present.

Culture Wars

As noted above, by the early 1990s, service learning as a pedagogy had fully embraced diversity. Today, few courses with a service component do not celebrate diversity, demand respect for "difference," or genuflect to equal status relationships between those who serve and the communities served. Diversity is also a necessity in terms of student recruitment into service opportunities. A program with appeal only to privileged, white students would be viewed as remiss in its obligations to both students and the communities served. The well-known "Principles of Good Practice" for service learning, the outcome of a Wingspread/Johnson Foundation conference, includes a mandate for diversity. A quality service learning program "is committed to program participation by and with diverse populations."[12] A recent publication of Campus Compact, an organization of college and university presidents committed to service as an aspect of higher education, includes articles and syllabi infused with diversity, as a concern and as a pedagogical opportunity.[13] For example, consider: "Teaching About Philanthropy and Service in an Academic Setting and Building a Community of Difference," "Community Service and Intercultural Education," "Campus-Community Collaboration," "Community Research in a Multicultural Context," and "American Literacy and Cultural Diversity."

Syllabi regularly remind students that nothing is simple once you enter civil society in the 1990s. A most articulate introduction to service learning is in a syllabus to a course on social responsibility. It places the student right in the middle of diversity and points in the direction of potential cultural war and the problem of language as both bridge and barrier. From the course summary and philosophy:

> This course revolves around the proposition that to be 'socially responsible' is not as simple as willing to be so. It is not simple because every significant concept embedded in our course topic is contested. It is not simple because one person's source of outrage over injustice can be someone else's "sacred order," about which there is nothing to be done except whatever one chooses to do with things "that just are." It is not simple, because one group's view of "doing good" may be another's "oppression." It is not simple, because the presence or absence of certain people's voices, what they experience and how they converse (literally) about issues connected to our course topic can shape the kinds of questions we raise and conclusions we draw.[14]

This course invited students to participate in social actions not typical of service learning courses: engaging in community conversations, bearing witness, and hearing and receiving stories. However, it does raise the essential issues embedded in all service learning. That is, that doing good, serving in American civil society in the 1990s, means the assertion of some version of a valued society and the suppression of another version or versions. Further, as this course makes clear, the cat is pretty much out of the bag. Any service learning educator quickly confronts the role education plays in suppressing and licensing voices once students begin bringing those voices back into the classroom. The confidence academics may have in their disciplinary orientation is challenged by the essential complexity of experience. The world as lived does not present itself as neatly as in a controlled study amenable to the cherished concepts, theories, and methods of one's discipline. But even recognizing the richer methodologies generated within the social sciences and humanities (and, occasionally, the natural sciences) in response to the claims of contemporary diversity, the educator with students in the world is painfully aware that there is no easy consensus on what we know that helps students make sense of experience and disposes them to action.

The culture wars seemingly fought on the ivy barricades of the academy have authorized or at least recognized a cacophony in the world as lived. The seemingly most advanced theoretical claims issuing from the academy cast into doubt the very possibility of objective knowledge of social or even natural processes. The world as lived by actual persons has always been more resistant to ordering, and more diverse in its frameworks, than our rhetoric of either positivistic social science or patriotic "we're all Americans here" acknowledged. But that diversity was partly masked by the concept of the private and the notion of individual exceptionalism. Holding to private "differences" and public or statistical uniformity has increasingly become viewed by some as a form of cowardice at the level of character and naiveté at the level of method.

Even as the meaning of a general American identity, a distinctive character, loses its unitary aspect and explodes into battalions of "others" at war, (i.e., identity politics,) service invites students to reconcile the claim that all persons be respected based upon common human identity with radical assumptions regarding the insurmountability of difference. Service initiates students into the epistemological and moral crisis at the center of contemporary collective life: your history can never overlap with mine, we speak a language so different as to defy translation, there is finally no stable world we can know or share.

Most service learning courses are modest in what they claim they are doing as regards diversity, cultural difference, and epistemology. Most attempt to honor universalism and diversity in ways that do not undermine faith in the possibility of some day rediscovering an essential American commonalty, if not character. The impact of service learning on student capacity for political judgment in such a context will be discussed below. Nonetheless, students themselves frequently provide moving testimony to the discovery that people originally viewed as alien, and even frightening, become with time and care "just like me," or rather, might have become just like me if they had had similar "opportunities."

A language of fate, bad luck, or fortuitous birth, has served our polity well as a discourse of dignity. The service learning movement in its mainstream practice provides this end run around essentialist differences and cultural war. In the presence of anger and rage and denial of similarity, young students somehow discover fellow citizens. Of course, the guided reflection and the learning in service learning are responsible in part for making sure this happens. No educator is pleased if a young woman or man asserts the last day of class that, "Those people are just like I thought, lazy, self-defeating victim mongers." If only because the "those" is too inclusive and undermines even right-wing claims that some can make it in America.

Service learning experiences and courses differentially place students on the battlefronts or in the rear guard of the culture wars. A course organized around AIDS may profoundly transform heterosexual students' assumptions regarding who gay people are and the culture they create and sustain. It may help them discover that some battles are worth fighting. Other courses, however, may invite students only to salute the rituals of cultural difference in the abstract, placing students in activities which are not in practice sensitive to differing cultural sensibilities.

Service learning in the context of identity and culture is in some ways well-suited to the traditional college-aged young person.[15] Experimenting with identity is almost a mandate for young college students. Developmentally, college may be the best time to introduce culture wars and identity politics, or even to present students with the grim aspects of colonialism, patriarchy, racism, homophobia, and Western cultural hegemony. They've lived in civil society, they know some of the story, and have seen some of the consequences. Yet what identity politics cannot do is what older social criticism did, that is, ask fundamental questions of political economy: has that economy formed the basis of any good life? Any communal identity? Any type of citizenship? Any society worth valuing? Service learning cannot finally prepare students for political action unless it addresses the most concrete level of social life, the material, and the most abstract level, the macro institutional order.[16]

The Material and Macro Bases of a Valued Society

It comes as no surprise that service learning may be less helpful as a mode of civic education with regard to economic class. Surely this is not because students do not meet poor people. Many programs and courses are organized solely around service to the "underprivileged" if not just plain poor. However, here is where we must return to the issue of level of analysis and experience. At the beginning of this chapter, I observed that service learning introduces students to society through the micro interactions of individuals in social contexts, the communal dynamics of cultures, groups, and communities, and the macro level of society and its institutions as bounded by the legal borders of our political community.

Diversity and culture wars are, in part, the outcome of macro forces, and, reciprocally, the micro processes and interactions of everyday life both reflect and constitute the macro.[17] I realize that claiming this places me immediately into a suspect category, especially with those postmodern theorists deeply skeptical of concepts, like social structure and macro forces, that seem to reify society and make it more solid than the free-flowing, disruptive, and negotiated social worlds they posit. Nonetheless, I believe that the rage or demoralization or friendliness of the individuals whom students meet as individuals in their service work is the outcome not only of personal experience but also of the language of accountability and justice deployed by the person served. Such a language drifts into and out of the big picture, and reflects assumptions themselves informed by abstract macro concepts such as state, justice, and membership. In short, in our society identity is partly constituted in the dialogue over what sort of society I live in, how it operates, and the resources I have access to based upon its workings.

Even if our big picture is elusive, never as cleanly outlined as social scientists once hoped, we must confront, as educators and citizens, the reality that, given the way we organize and legitimate our society, some flourish in embarrassing excess while others suffer for want of simple things. And most people have some understanding of why.

Reducing social action only to the micro interactions between individuals does confer agency, and with it a certain dignity and power to the individuals in interaction. Yes, any individual can dramatically change the world for another through murder, and for a nation through assassination. More benignly, through service to one person, a young person may feel empowered. I have heard many, many times the claim that the big picture is too confusing or tiresome or demoralizing, but "If I can help just one (fill in ... underprivileged child, older person, person with AIDS) I've done something." The experience becomes even more empowering if the person helped began by hating you because you were from a different culture, or because you were rich or ... and ended up accepting your humanity and offer of friendship. At a time when good will is not in excess, such small dramas of reconciliation are moving beyond their modesty.

However, the reason why we find them so moving also might point to the context within which micro decencies seem to demand our respect and attention while macro injustices go ignored. My argument will move in two directions from this point. I will begin by focusing on the material and physical context within which service takes place, and then return to the necessity for macro analysis if we are to create a service learning approach that is profoundly political.

Material Context

In the West, scarcity of the physical prerequisites for a decent life has been the focus of social criticism and reform for much of the modern era. This statement is not meant to reduce critical social and political thought to a crude materialism. On the contrary, both critics and general theorists of modernity recognize that the evolution of a market economy, the democratization of institutions, and the rationalization of nature led to new demands on the part of heretofore invisible persons that the quality of their lives were or should be of concern to the state. Although classical liberalism as the dominant political ideology attendant on the above transformations was resistant to any universal notion of what a good life entailed (indeed, that was and is its charm for many even today), it did support a vision of the person as having *a* claim on a good life, here on earth, as soon as possible if not today. Initially, the market was to provide that good life, that is, to generate an unending series of opportunities both to deploy one's labor and amass one's goods in the interest of constructing a life worth living.

Today, late industrial and post-industrial capitalism may still offer such opportunities for many but surely not for all. More frightening is the growing perception that it offers such opportunities for ever fewer. Service learning is the context where many young people first encounter the way the world of late capitalism "works" and its consequences.

Ironically, the very intellectual moves that have forced women, gays, and post-colonial peoples into the view of other people in societies have also made it more difficult to explore how the physical and material world gets constituted. Old-time leftists viewed labor as the nodal point of their critical analysis. Labor, at least in early capitalism, was easy to envision, its rewards and punishments easy to witness. The abstract nature of much contemporary labor and the denigration of remaining physical work have made it more difficult to assess who is overly burdened by the labor they must do to create the basis for her or his good life.

Further, it appears as if we (including Western democracies in general) may not be able to absorb all members of our polity(ies) into civil society through paid work. The institutions that once kept persons out of the work force—unpaid motherhood, homemaking, and volunteerism, disability, or lack of skills—are no longer viewed as legitimate reasons not to be employed. This is happening at the very time when the heretofore marginalized groups are claiming recognition for labors once simply invisible. Much of that invisible labor was social labor; the efforts of women and other marginalized groups to sustain social worlds and their members, whether families or communities or nations.

What has this to do with service learning? I would argue that service learning is in part about teaching young people how to perform social and invisible labor.[18] However, as with women before them, student volunteers are not encouraged to consider their labors as political; as constitutive of civil society, ratified by legal status, and reflective of the distribution of power and resources. In short, just as with women who were the hidden human capital that allowed a family to launch a father or son into the marketplace, student volunteers are the brigades of the good patching up a rapidly fraying social fabric so that the contradictions in the production, organization, and distribution of material goods do not overwhelm and destabilize our political community.

Students do drift into this insight and become politicized, but it is not on the official agenda. Indeed, the Corporation for National and Community Service, for obviously prudential and legal reasons, reminds potential grantees that activities that could mobilize students to confront the material organization of production and consumption are not to be supported with federal money. Under prohibited service, the first three listed are:

- any effort to influence legislation, as prohibited under 501 (c) of the Internal Revenue Code of 1986 (26 U.S.C. 501 (c));

- organizing protests, petitions, boycotts, or strikes;

- assisting, promoting, or deterring union organizing.[19]

These are not surprising prohibitions. Change agents at the local level trying to act locally but think globally are not an easy sell, especially given local experience with initial VISTA volunteers and the Community Action Programs of the Johnson years.[20]

Of course, many faculty with or without federal support, do include a macro analysis of social problems that does focus on the material and class basis of society in service learning courses, and do, intentionally or not, create an environment conducive to political action, at least on the part of some students. However, the movement to political judgment and action is not easy, because macro analysis itself is not easy given the erosion of grand theory, criticism of the hubris implied by a positive social science, and recognition of the socially constructive labors behind any factual claim about the world.

The Challenge of Macro Analysis

It is difficult to defend macro analysis given the intellectual moves made under the banner of post-structuralism and postmodernism as they fuse with feminism and post-colonial analysis of Western intellectual hegemony. Still more difficult is it to insist that a college sophomore pay attention to macro trends in homelessness and a functional analysis of poverty when a person she has come to know is hungry and cold tonight.

For purposes of clarity, I am using the sociologist Randall Collins's definitions of macro and micro as used by sociologists. Sociology is the social science where issues of method and level of analysis are perhaps the most sophisticated:

> Microsociology is the detailed analysis of what people do, say, and think in the actual flow of momentary experience. Macrosociology is the analysis of larger-scale and long term social processes, often treated as self-subsistent entities such as 'state,' 'organization,' 'class,' 'economy,' 'culture,' and 'society.'[21]

The phenomenology of working with actual persons and communities in need or in crisis may create the conditions whereby any attempt to move young people to macro analysis and potential political action based upon that analysis is perceived as heartless or useless. Why is this so? Why does the experience of serving encourage for many a suspicion of intellectual and cognitive analysis if it is not grounded in the moment of experience?

Let us begin with the issue of identity explored above. One dominant critique of Western thought has been its presumed dualisms. In short and in the context of service, a young person is invited to transcend dualisms—theory versus practice, emotion versus reason, individual versus society—that have been the ordering armatures of Western thought. She is enjoined to engage herself in the world as a full person, right now. True, this full person may suddenly be confronted with "others" whose own identity is at considerable variance with her assumptions about how persons ought to live their lives. However, sensitivity to diversity and cultural subtleties, encouraged in the classroom will prepare (at least it is hoped) such a student to act with sensitivity in the community. Part of that sensitivity includes the recognition that other cultures place differential value on cognitive, interactional, emotional, esthetic, or communal capacities. Indeed, students are frequently invited to use "other ways of knowing" as new sources of insight into the lived world. In such a context, traditional disciplines and theory must appear inadequate, narrow, and partial; particularly macro theories that name processes that other cultures refuse to recognize as part of their spatial and temporal context.

Postmodern orientations provide more adequate means of addressing the phenomenology of the service experience. With guidance, students can discover in service that identity is indeed fluid, classifications do break down and are reconstructed, persons are socially situated and their positions not rooted in fundamental truths about human existence baptized by Western social science.

Mainstream service learning programs, however, do not usually explore the postmodern dimensions of service directly. Given the immediacy of the experience and its social and psychological demands, they may not have the time to help students understand how relevant the controversies at the frontiers of theory are to their service experience. To many students in mainstream service programs, the phenomenology of service includes a more visceral reaction to Western dualism; a deep anger that theorists, policy makers, intellectuals of all stripes, and politicians do not "walk their talk." A profound anti-intellectualism can attend service learning. Abstraction itself is the enemy, and action right now is the solution. Faculty supportive of service learning often become frustrated because students in turn do not "talk their walk." Students resist the very theory and statistics that some faculty believe are essential if students are to envision civil society in a way that can lead to policy judgments and social change.

Students are impatient with tracing the history or social construction of a social problem. They may not wish to struggle with the complexity involved in questioning how data sets are amassed or how accurate they are. They may not wish to unravel how the problem they care so much about became visible to them, how need was defined, and whether a language of need masks political and economic power. The very language of service presumes care and concern, not disengaged analysis. Traditional Western dualisms work well in this context to de-legitimate large scale analysis of how systems and institutions work.

Nonetheless, the tensions explored in the social sciences between agency and structure are at the center of the service learning experience. Micro and qualitative approaches to social life are much more congenial to young people looking for agency in themselves and in the communities and persons they serve than macro, abstract, and theoretically dense explanations for how the larger, even global, political economy works. Such micro perspectives and qualitative methods, and those of postmodernism, may provide comfort to the young person whose intellectual plate, everyday life, and service experience are filled with the dramas of social interaction and identity politics.

Finally, there is the issue of usefulness. For example, macro analysis of globalizing financial markets and their constraints on opportunities in political communities, both advanced postindustrial ones and those still agricultural, may well lead to despair. Such macro analysis is very hard work, or at least it is presented as so arcane and complex that ordinary persons, even students in higher education, are unable to envision the structure of a global human society or trace its processes. It is one thing to interact with people with very different assumptions about a good life. It is another to imagine how a human global order can generate the material basis for such diversity or assess why it has not.

Under such circumstances, it is understandable why young people in service may come to view large-scale issues of political economy as akin to the weather. Students are not foolish. They understand that claims for social justice enhanced by the rhetoric of diversity demand that there be more opportunities for some and perhaps fewer for others. Yet the economy and its operations have become so opaque that many students and citizens accept the consequences of those operations on each others' lives, try to do the best they can to help everyone survive, and view "fancy" abstract theory as more relevant to theological disputation than the material circumstances of their lives. The thought of one more study while people suffer today drives many young people to despair of action at any level beyond the most easily envisioned.

The question remains whether citizens in general have the capacity for the macro analysis necessary to comprehend what large-scale social change would actually entail. Service learning could be a crucible to test whether citizens could be initiated into such an inquiry. Students in service discover the stakes of such an inquiry, but their call to care, the need for their invisible labor to make all of us believe that action *is* being taken and good things *are* being accomplished, gets us all off the hook. If we attend to identity, diversity, and multicultural dignity, must we also ask about investment policy and capital flow? In a heterogeneous society the maintenance of civil society consumes vast human energy; energy that is siphoned away from political and economic analysis. When the social fabric shreds, we have the social psychology of the talk show to assure us that it is not the economy that is at issue even though numbers of damaged souls speak of losing jobs, no money, and having to leave family and friends in search of work paying a living wage. When the social fabric shreds, we also have cadres of young people offering individuals and communities their "summer of service" and "summer of safety."

Will service learning ever become political? Not civic, in the bland or safe sense, but political in its concern with power and justice, not just in the micro world of prisoners and inmates but the macro world where life settings—indeed, whole cultures—are allowed to flourish or die as a result of impersonal investment strategies? In the past, the material bases for cultures have been destroyed regardless of the glory of their languages, the charm of their gods, and the pleasing nature of their rituals.

If the service learning movement does become increasingly political, service learning will become wildly contested as to its practice and its pedagogy. It will also reach out to new or at least different theoretical orientations. But it will never become so until it grapples with the question of political economy, and not merely at the level of the nation state. Localized economic development strategies point to the direction such an analysis may take. Students and the communities they serve, come to know, and appreciate may be driven to such analysis once identity politics confronts scarcity.

It would be easier all around if at the level of our political community we were able to specify what material resources we need in order to live a life worth living. If we had agreed-upon standards it would be much easier to hold our political and economic institutions accountable for achieving those standards.

While we argue over dress and mores, language and respect, religion and ritual, the material world of production and consumption drifts away from the command of citizens. We must return to questions of its accountability. If we wait too long, the material basis of our lives will collapse back into a seeming state of nature. We will indeed be incapable of understanding that human agency is infinitely complex, expressed in institutions that are, finally, of human origin, supported and legitimated by language and through practice, including the practices of mercy and the small decencies of service.

Conclusion

If we are to make the service experience an opportunity for young people to examine critically how our civil society is ordered, we must find a way to balance the immediacy of compassion with an inquiry into the material basis of good lives and valued persons. It may be that compassion is the harder task, and so that is the vineyard in which service learning advocates work. Learning to recognize that "others" unlike ourselves are human may be the great, noble task of our times. However, an unwillingness to view persons as data, as the residue of the workings of social structure and institutions, can lead to a variety of political stances, from doing nothing to revolution. People in their dignity may sleep under bridges. It is only when we ask about life chances, what people eat and why, where people live and why, how people work and what they do and why, who dies and who lives and why, who lingers in prison or goes to prep school and why, that we begin to assess whether our civil society, legitimated by the formal processes of democracy, is a just polity. To answer those questions we need to think at a level that seems to diminish the passions and immediacy of experience. Yet, if diversity and cultural war do not lead us back to questions of justice rooted in the basics of health and want, hunger and satiation, pleasure and suffering, life and death, birth and birth weight, we will indeed be relieved of the burden of asking whether we live in a just and good society ordered by a legitimate political regime. We will not have to act politically, forge pragmatic alliances, or join social movements.

Justice, goodness, legitimacy, the meaning of political are all contested. More so now that we have accepted that diversity is and will be the basis of whatever society the future holds. We do not yet know to what degree the service experience has led students from a respect for difference and an appreciation for a variety of cultures into political action or social movements.[22] We do not know if students have found in complex macro theory a way to envision what political action should entail. We can hope that in coming to know others unlike themselves, students and communities have broadened their understanding of who must be considered when political action, grounded in an analysis of political economy, *is* taken. Perhaps this awareness that the stakes and consequences of political action must include their impact on persons once invisible to me but now present in my heart and memory as I act as citizen is the long term, and blessedly unanticipated, consequence of service learning.

NOTES

1. Not all supporters of service learning focus on its civically educative potential. There are many reasons to advocate for service learning. See, for example, Jane C. Kendall and Associates, *Combining Service and Learning: A Resource Book for Community and Public Service Volumes I and II*, (Raleigh, North Carolina: National Society for Internships and Experiential Education, 1990) for a full range of these reasons. However, even the recently constituted Corporation on National and Community Service recognizes the *civic potential* of service learning, emphasizing it in its publications and using the civically educational potential of a program as a criterion for awarding grants. Further, one of the most innovative service learning programs in the country, at Rutgers University, is fully civic. See Benjamin Barber and Richard Battistoni, editors, *Education for Democracy: Citizenship, Community and Service* (Dubuque, Iowa: Kendall/ Hunt, 1994).

2. David Thorton Moore, "Experiential Education as Critical Discourse," in Kendall, ed., *Combining Service and Learning*, pp. 273–283.

3. For a subtle and controversial discussion of the idea of civil society, see Adam Seligman, *The Idea of Civil Society* (New York: The Free Press, 1992).

4. See William F. Buckley, *Gratitude: Reflections on What We Owe Our Country* (New York: Random House, 1990).

5. See Cornel West, "The New Cultural Politics of Difference," in *Higher Education and the Practice of Democratic Politics*, Bernard Murchland, ed., (Dayton, Ohio: The Kettering Foundation, 1991) for a postmodern defense of "difference" as the most compelling approach to contemporary cultural and social criticism.

6. See Manuel Ramirez and Alfredo Castaneda, "Toward Cultural Democracy," in Murchland, 1991, for an analysis of language as a dominant consideration in contemporary democratic practice.

7. *Ibid.*, pp. 118–120.

8. R. Freeman Butts, *The Revival of Civic Learning*, (Bloomington, Indiana: Phi Delta Kappan Educational Foundation, 1980).

9. Richard Hofstadter, *The Age of Reform* (New York: Random House, 1955).

10. See Addams's essay, "A Modern King Lear," in Christopher Lasch, ed., *The Social Thought of Jane Addams* (Indianapolis: Bobbs-Merrill, 1965).

11. See Jane Addams, *The Spirit of Youth and City Streets* (Urbana: University of Illinois Press, 1972).

12. Suzanne W. Morse, *Renewing Civic Capacity* (Washington, D.C.:ERIC, 1989), p.43.

13. See Tamar Y. Kupiec, ed., *Rethinking Tradition: Integrating Service with Academic Study on College Campuses* (Denver: Education Commission of the States, 1993).

14. *Ibid.*, p. 170.

15. This chapter focuses upon traditional college-age students. More and more students in higher education are non "traditional" in terms of age, culture, or social class. Service learning that includes such student populations is a complex enterprise; identity to non-traditional students may be an even more compelling concern than it is to traditional college-age students. However, I believe my analysis of service learning holds even given this phenomenon. If anything, a more diverse student body generates more concern regarding diversity and cultural differences than does a homogeneous student body. One reason for the focus on diversity in higher education is that college campuses themselves are mini-polities confronted with growing diversity in their own civil societies.

16. For a defense of difference as the *most* potent basis for political action, see Iris Marion Young, *Justice and the Politics of Difference* (Princeton: Princeton University Press, 1990).

17. For an analysis of the relationship between micro and macro sociology, see Gary Alan Fine, "On the Macrofoundations of Microsociology: Constraint and the Exterior Reality of Structure," *Sociological Quarterly* 32, no. 2 (1991): 161–177.

18. See, Eric B. Gorman, *National Service, Citizenship and Political Education* (Albany: State University of New York, 1992), Chapter 6, for another interpretation of the role of service in an increasingly "service economy."

19. The Corporation for National and Community Service, *Learn and Serve America: Application Materials,* 1994, p.10.

20. See Joseph A. Califano, *The Triumph and Tragedy of Lyndon Johnson* (New York: Simon & Schuster, 1991), Chapter 4, for a discussion of the resistance to the social change possibilities inherent in both VISTA and the Office of Economic Opportunity.

21. Randall Collins, "On the Microfoundations of Macrosociology," in *American Journal of Sociology* 86, no. 5 (March 1981): 984–1014.

22. There are some suggestions regarding the link between service learning and political action in the evolution of the student-based national organization, COOL, Campus Outreach Opportunity League. Recently, COOL has become more critical of service learning activities that do not lend themselves to eventual activism. The form such activism might take is still unclear.

Joan N. Burstyn

Chapter 10

Meeting the Demands of
Postmodern Society

Introduction

In this chapter, I consider how three interlocking characteristics of contemporary life in the United States influence what it means to be a valuable member of our society. These three characteristics make necessary, for both children and adults, a new kind of education, embedded in our everyday life at work and at home, through informal as well as formal educational institutions. The three characteristics are: the complex demands of society on each individual; the extensive use of space and communications technology, particularly networked computer-video technology; and the drive to maintain within society both pluralism and equity. These characteristics are not exclusive to the United States. They are shared, increasingly, by other industrialized countries through the global economy.

There is a tension in our need to think in both particularistic and universal terms about the problems identified below. According to David Hollinger, when modernist scholars earlier in the century thought in universal terms, they did so without reflecting on the limitations of their own perspective.[1] A dilemma that postmodern thought produces for me is that while it has, indeed, made me conscious of the limitations of my own location and time, and of the dangers of generalizing from the experience of one's own culture, it has not led me to abandon a belief that certain activities, such as the participation of citizens in the government of their country, are universally "good," or at least universally "better" than citizens' non-participation. In this chapter, therefore, I want to acknowledge "the limits of the [moral and] epistemic 'we' "[2] in discussing what it means to be a citizen, in order to avoid distinctions and exclusions that have oppressed individuals and groups in the past, while advocating the need for a vision of citizenship that, in some ways, is universal. These issues will be discussed again later.

The complex demands of society on each individual, the extensive use of space and communications technology, and the drive to maintain within society both pluralism and equity are often experienced by us simultaneously. Authors I quote often wrote with an intense urgency just because they had experienced these characteristics at the same moment, and had been overwhelmed by their implications. Although I sometimes discuss the characteristics separately, I intend to minimize the separation among them in the discussion below.

181

Civic Responsibilities in the Complex World of Today

Although we may not often admit it, many of us feel overburdened by our day-to-day activities. We have little time or inclination to take on civic responsibilities. Elsewhere in this book, James and Ellen Giarelli have described the ways that our so-called public schools teach us how to excel at activities benefiting ourselves as individuals. Schools give scant attention to teaching students the skills they need to build a community, or to maintain its well-being. Fay Kelle has described the decline of participation in our democratic governance system. She proposes ways to change this situation through critical pedagogy. Barbara McEwan, mindful of the violence plaguing our society, has described how schools can model a way to live peaceably. I will add that among the causes of our current malaise lie the complex demands that life in society today makes on each of us.

In this discussion, I include not only the interactions of our daily lives, but also the significance of global affairs on our lives, and the demands put upon us to act on behalf of people in countries other than our own. When we consider what it will mean to be a valuable citizen in the future, we need to question the very basis of our assumptions about citizenship. With satellites transmitting images across the world as they occur, with many people employed by international companies, and with all of us linked across continents by electronic networks, to whom does each of us owe allegiance? And for what purposes? We may have to consider multiple allegiances in the future, since most people belong to many communities at once, and have to divide their time and labor among them.[3] One of those communities is surely a worldwide community linked not only technologically but also morally. Political analysts have long believed that people find difficulty retaining allegiance to large-scale communities (as Mauhs-Pugh suggests elsewhere in this volume). Recently, Andrew Oldenquist, following a tradition in the United States dating at least from Alexander Hamilton, suggests that "equal moral concern for the whole of humanity or the whole sentient nature is, for most of us, too diluted to be able to generate effective moral enthusiasm and too weak to outweigh narrower loyalties."[4] The questions above, about our allegiances and our obligations, are usually not asked. Only when we are faced by the threat of international conflict do they become important.

We sometimes assume that the impact of nuclear weapons on international affairs has caused us to look for new ways of thinking and new approaches to diplomacy in order to avoid war. But the increased dangers of war predated the advent of nuclear weapons. Maria Montessori, writing during the 1930s, spoke of the futility of war and the need for "a new man" [and woman] who might conceive of ways to use new technologies for the benefit of humankind rather than its destruction.

In poetic, almost visionary, language that seems alien to the data-based language of social scientists today, Montessori identified a crisis that "can be compared only to one of those biological or geological epochs in which new, higher, more perfect forms of life appeared, as totally new conditions on earth came about." She warned that "If man remains earth-bound and unconscious of the new realities, if he uses the energies of space for the purpose of destroying himself, he will soon attain that goal, for the energies now at his disposal are immeasurable and accessible to everyone, at all times and in every corner of the earth."[5]

Her plan was to develop a new form of education for the child, to produce an adult able to function in the new conditions. "Two things are necessary: the development of individuality and the participation of the individual in a truly social life. The development and this participation in social activities will take different forms in the various periods of childhood. But one principle will remain unchanged during all these stages: the child must be furnished at all times with the means necessary for him [or her] to act and gain experience. His [or her] life as a social being will then develop throughout his [or her] formative years, becoming more and more complex as he [or she] grows older."[6] Thus, Montessori foresaw the need for children to construct their own ways of knowing through action, and sought to facilitate the growth of complexity in children's knowledge of how to handle social relations. Montessori's constructivist approach to education echoes John Dewey's comment that "the ethical responsibility of the school on the social side must be interpreted in the broadest and freest spirit; it is equivalent to that training of the child which will give him [or her] such possession of himself that he may take charge of himself; may not only adapt himself to the changes that are going on, but have power to shape and direct them."[7] Each of these ideas is an important component of the education of citizens for tomorrow's world. However, in order for an individual to have the power to shape and direct changes in his or her environment, as Dewey and Montessori envisioned, I believe that additional insights are necessary. I would add the need for students to understand the processes of production and exchange that take place during teaching and learning, and the implications for both teacher and learner of the differences in their respective power. Students need, also, to learn about the differences in power among people of different age, gender, race, and class. Differences in power affect the curriculum, the methods of teaching and learning, the exchanges that take place during the process of teaching and learning, and the nature of the knowledge created by the learner.[8]

Some decades after Montessori had written the words quoted above, Marshall McLuhan echoed her understanding of the vast impact on the world of technological change. He described a concept of world citizenship: Earth as a global village brought into being through the diffusion of radio, video, and film; the global village entailing concern in each of us for the welfare of other people throughout the world.[9] According to McLuhan, the media are themselves the message: how we understand the world is shaped by the media available to us. Our understanding changes as new media develop.[10] Although as a historian I am hesitant to draw this conclusion, I think it may be possible for new media to cause people to need more complex ways of thinking and acting than they have ever needed before. Were we to conclude that our current technology had already led us that far, then great changes in the education of boys and girls, and men and women, would be called for.

The challenge to develop more complex ways of thinking and acting than men and women have ever used before could possibly prove too great for a society to meet. As I write this, I recall the eighteenth-century historian Edward Gibbon, in *The Decline and Fall of the Roman Empire*, and the twentieth-century historian Arnold Toynbee, in *A Study of History*. Both sought explanations for the systemic failure of societies.[11] Toynbee's thesis of challenge and response suggests that, although societies continuously face challenges which they overcome by appropriate responses, they may encounter a challenge so intense that they are overwhelmed by it. Challenges to a society may be military ones, but they may also be—perhaps at one and the same time—environmental or, as in this case, mental challenges that result from previously unknown technologies. To gauge whether a technology demands of people more complex ways of thinking and acting than humans have *ever* needed before would be nearly impossible. Within a given society, however, a new technology may demand of people different, and in some cases more complex, ways of thinking and acting than the historical record suggests have ever been demanded before.

Implications of the Growing Complexity of Contemporary Life

In the United States, we are committed to both the maintenance of liberal democracy and the efficacy of technological innovation. We are loath, therefore, to consider the possibility that human beings are capable of designing a society too complex for the majority to survive in, or at least too complex for the majority to feel comfortable in. We are even less willing to contemplate the possibility that our own society might be reaching that level of complexity. Instead, we commit ourselves to improving our educational institutions to meet new challenges as they occur.

"A democracy requires twin goals for education from which there can be no retreat. Schools must be both equal and excellent. Equality in education is predicated on the belief that in a democracy all citizens are entitled to the skills necessary for thoughtful and active citizenship."[12] Therefore, if society is becoming more complex and people need new and previously unforseen skills in order to participate fully in it, our task is to redesign our educational institutions to ensure that everyone has the opportunity to learn those new skills.

I think it is worthwhile to consider the unspeakable idea that humans can design a society too complex for the majority to feel comfortable in, if only to examine the implications of such a suggestion for the education of future citizens and the institutions they construct. Some rebellions, such as the Luddites' unsuccessful attacks on factories in nineteenth-century England, or the successful attack by Islamic religious leaders on the Iranian government of the Shah in the 1970s, may be explained from social, economic, and political perspectives. However, they could also be interpreted as revolts against the complexity of society by those whose ways of knowing were different in kind from those of the people in power.

Such an interpretation might lead one to hypothesize differently about the conditions that lead to rebellions, such as those mentioned above, and the ways they might be avoided in the future. In this respect, Robert Kegan's theories, described below, can be used to explain the "flaws in human nature" that Arnold Toynbee, in the 1930s, hypothesized undermined every civilization sooner or later. As summarized recently by his biographer William H. McNeill, Toynbee argued that "in different places and times, human beings had accepted the restraints and benefits of civilization for a while, but only as long as 'creative minorities' succeeded in meeting successive challenges so successfully as to be able to attract willing assent of their fellows to whatever innovative actions they advocated. But persistent flaws in human nature meant that sooner or later, the growth of every recorded civilization had been checked by the unleashed brutality of war."[13]

The Need for a More Sophisticated Way of Knowing

Why is society now so complex that people feel overwhelmed? Discussions of other topics, such as the reform of the health care and welfare systems, often deal tangentially with the question. Politicians sometimes attempt to simplify governmental structures and even to reduce the paperwork demanded of clients and employees. Such attempts tinker with the institutions of society, fine-tune them, as it were, to make them work more efficiently, thereby lessening the frustration of individuals who have to interact with them. The source of people's frustration is perceived to lie merely in the inefficiency of the institutions they encounter. In such an analysis, Total Quality Management is what is called for.

Robert Kegan, in his recent book, *In Over Our Heads: the Mental Demands of Modern Life*, hypothesizes that, disparate though they may seem, the demands made on us in our society as adolescents and as adults, in our personal as well as our work lives, have much in common. Each demands a more complex *way of knowing* than has been demanded of people in former times. It is here, incidentally, that I find Kegan's assumptions most problematic. Without his theoretical framework to analyze diaries, letters, official documents, and other writings, we have no idea whether, and if so to what extent, people in the past ever used the complex way of knowing he claims we are required to use now. Nevertheless, his is a generative hypothesis. Kegan engages the ideas of several other authors, including those concerned with race and gender equity, who have, in recent years, challenged the assumptions of psychologists such as himself as race- and gender-biased.[14]

Kegan's conception of intellectual and psychosocial development is similar to that of other developmental psychologists, although his descriptive terms differ in some ways from theirs. Each of us moves in adolescence and early adulthood through what he calls the second order of consciousness, with its self-centered point of view and concern with concrete operations, to the third order, the order of cross-categorical meaning-making in which the individual can think in abstractions, reflect objectively on his or her own point of view, and engage in reciprocal interpersonal transactions. However, according to Kegan, the third order of consciousness no longer suffices for adults, who are called upon more and more frequently to exercise a fourth order of consciousness, by means of which, according to Kegan, people create a system for choosing among their values when they conflict. This is a process by which a person "gathers cross-categorical constructions into a complex or integrated system."[15] Kegan goes on to suggest that even a fourth order of consciousness is insufficient for postmodern thought, which demands a fifth order of consciousness, by which people comprehend the relative nature of cross-categorical systems and the interdependence of "the self" and "the other" in any definition of the self, even in situations of conflict.[16]

Each of these orders of consciousness, then, affects a person in the cognitive, sociocognitive, and intrapersonal-affective domains. According to Kegan, any change in one's way of knowing is a *gradual* process, and therefore "it would be normal for people during perhaps much of their adolescence to be *unable* to meet the expectations the adult culture holds out for them!"[17] Few adults appear to understand that people adopt new ways of knowing only gradually. As a result, parents and teachers often demand more of an adolescent than he or she can deliver. The same holds for our expectations of other adults, be they our life partners or our work colleagues. While more is sometimes demanded of an adolescent than third-order cross-categorical meaning-making, an adult is *often* called upon to go beyond the third order. Kegan concludes that those whose ways of knowing are based in the third order of consciousness are more likely than those who have moved into the fourth order to feel as though they are in over their heads.

Kegan backs up this claim with the results of thirteen studies that used interview questions and answers to test his hypothesis. He concludes that the phenomenon of being "in over our heads" is widespread across socioeconomic and educational levels. When he examined a sample of only the most highly educated members of society, he still found "the phenomenon of being in over one's head remains widespread. Here, over half the sample has not fully reached the fourth order of consciousness."[18] If Kegan is correct, if modern life makes mental demands on many of us that we cannot comfortably meet, our society has a major problem.

One might argue that a person cannot be hurried from one order of consciousness to another, that he or she has to travel through many life experiences in order to gain perspective about them. At any one moment in time, according to this argument, there are bound to be many people in any society whose understanding is limited to Kegan's first three orders of consciousness, in part because there will be a fair proportion of young people in the population whose life experiences are still too limited for them to have moved to a fourth order of consciousness.

While in the past a small proportion of people did acquire a fourth order of consciousness through life experience, many did not. Would education, then, have facilitated their move from one order of consciousness to another? We cannot know the answer to this hypothetical question. All we know at the moment is that, according to a small sample of studies conducted in the United States and reported by Kegan, a majority of the most highly educated do *not* use his fourth order of consciousness to organize their lives. That finding, if replicated in other studies, would suggest that our current methods of education do *not* facilitate the change from the third to the fourth order of consciousness, at least for very many people. If Kegan is correct in his analysis that adults in our society are more and more often called upon to use a fourth or even a fifth order of consciousness, then educators will have to facilitate the evolution of such thinking in young adults. Such facilitation may come about, of course, in ways other than those conceived by Kegan.

Learning Democratic Practice in a Complex Society

While the notion of being "in over our heads" is basically psychological, Kegan's general thesis has been expressed in other ways. For example, programs in undergraduate education already underway at Alverno College in Milwaukee assume the need for students to develop complex, multidisciplinary abilities, including what is termed *perspective taking* and *valuing in decision making*. Courses in a variety of subjects have been designed to facilitate the learning of these skills, which seem akin to those possessed by Kegan's fourth-order thinkers. Without relying on Kegan's analysis, then, these programs facilitate in students the growth in ways of knowing that he advocates. Alverno College has years of experience in this kind of teaching and learning. The college has conducted an ongoing longitudinal assessment of its programs' effects using external assessors from the business and professional community.[19]

Shoshana Zuboff has described businesses where workers, often with great reluctance, have to acquire new ways of knowing. No longer able to rely on experience derived from their sense of touch, for example, paper makers have to learn to interpret computer-generated data. "The ability to engage in such analytical reasoning is complemented by an overarching theoretical conception of the processes to which the data refer. . . . Intellective competence at this level depends upon an explicit, consciously articulated theory that can provide a framework for data analysis."[20] Zuboff points out that such changes involve a reorientation of one's notion of how one influences the world.[21]

Kegan makes clear that his approach is not merely developmental. Ways of knowing are embedded, not only in the individual but also in the culture and its expectations. To illustrate this, he hypothesizes what he refers to as a Traditional community of the past, which, he claims, "represents one way in which the third order consciousness of individuals can be supported to resolve the fourth order tasks of adult life, such as those intrinsic to parenting."[22] Such a community rarely *tells* people what to do. Rather, the information is communicated "in the very fabric or ground of living." Such a community, however, is alien to the experience of most Americans today, Kegan argues. "Although it may constitute *one* form of 'borrowable mind' to support third order consciousness in the regulation of fourth order tasks, the essence of today's pluralistic, privatistic, individualistic, and secular modernity is to fragment the mental monolith of Tradition."[23] Hence, Americans, by and large, get no direction from the environment even though it imposes tasks of fourth order complexity on each of us.

I conclude from the above discussion of the influence of culture in shaping the demands placed on people that our culture may not need to demand of all individuals what it now demands of them. If society were differently organized, support from the community might help most individuals cope with fourth-order tasks for which they may not be mentally equipped. Society would then not need to insist that each individual, or as many individuals as possible, attain a fourth-order way of knowing. Instead, it would ensure that supports were available, on an equitable basis, for its people to carry out their fourth-order tasks.

Such a solution, however, smacks of authoritarianism and a denial of individual agency, both of which are anathema to a democratic society. Thus, for example, standardization becomes a source of conflict when it limits individual rights, even when the majority might benefit, say, from the standardization of computer equipment or of applications to reimburse medical costs. Another problem is that, if one believes that American society has become a more sophisticated and mature democracy as the years have passed, one looks on Kegan's mythical Traditional society as less mature and less desirable than the society of today. We are not likely, therefore, to turn the clock back to provide more individuals with the kind of societal supports they had formerly. Despite these concerns, it might be possible, using Edward de Bono's lateral thinking,[24] or other creative problem-solving techniques, to develop ways that our sophisticated democratic society might simplify its organization to decrease the intellectual demands on its citizens.

As Kegan describes it, however, the dilemma facing society is not one of restructuring society so that a less complex series of tasks faces each individual. Rather, we must change our processes of education, formal and informal, to facilitate the development of more complex ways of knowing and ensure that these ways are developed early in life among an overwhelming majority of the individuals in the population.

To achieve this goal, we need to think of life's experiences as its curriculum. Our culture shapes that curriculum. For instance, our culture makes "a widespread demand for a common transformation of mind during adolescence" from categorical to cross-categorical ways of knowing. Adolescents may be taught so as to encourage the mental stretch they must make to glimpse the new ways of knowing.[25] Society might also institute new curricula for adults, to ensure both pluralism and gender and race equity.

From a psychological perspective, Kegan's description of modern society echoes the analysis made by Robert Bellah, Richard Madsen, William Sullivan, Ann Swidler, and Steven Tipton, in *Habits of the Heart*.[26] Both Bellah *et al.* and Kegan address the atomization of society, the privatization of ambition, and the decline of community. But, where Bellah *et al.* concentrate on the social and political implications of these phenomena, Kegan concentrates on their psychological implications for the individual.

In this respect, Kegan's theory appears profoundly conservative. He seeks to change the individual's understanding of their situation rather than to change the situation itself. Distancing oneself from one's experiences, reflecting on them, and analyzing them are intellectual, not action-focused activities. Donald Schön makes a nice distinction between reflection-*on*-action and reflection-*in*-action, claiming that professionals need both to perform their work.[27] Kegan does not make that distinction, although both forms of reflection could be used by people who act according to either third- or fourth-order ways of knowing. Kegan's examples of fourth-order thinking suggest that people who use that complex way of knowing accept ambiguities and contradictions that third-order thinkers would find intolerable and seek to resolve through social or individual action.

Psychoanalysis persuaded suburban homemakers in the 1950s to perceive their anxieties as neuroses coming from themselves, rather than from social problems affecting homemakers as a group and located in the structure of suburban life and the ideology of gender relations.[28] So Kegan's analysis, despite his claims that it is non-judgmental, locates the problem of being "in over our heads" within the individual who has not yet learned an appropriately complex way of knowing.

From another perspective, however, Kegan's theory offers the individual new tools for engaging in social action. The political actions of many people today reflect third-order thinking, according to which they understand the points of view of other people but cannot envision a pattern inclusive of that point of view and their own. Thus, people become "stuck" at an early stage of negotiation, too impatient to wait for positive results they cannot foresee. Although Kegan does not develop this idea, a fourth order of consciousness is likely to enable people to resolve conflicts more readily.

In the context of conflicts, the work of Edward de Bono provides an alternative mechanism for facilitating change. In becoming stuck in their negotiations, people are unable to move into what de Bono has described as lateral thinking.[29] Lateral thinking frees one to suggest and then play with alternatives that are "unthinkable" because they seem illogical, or counter-rational.

Unlike Kegan, de Bono speaks with an urgency similar to Montessori's in an earlier time, and for the same reason: fear that the weapons devised by technological enterprise will threaten the whole of civilization unless men and women learn to interact peaceably:

> We do have to accept that our methods of solving disputes and conflicts are crude and primitive, inadequate and costly, dangerous and destructive.
>
> Even if we operate these methods with the best will in the world and with the highest intelligence, they will not suffice. There is a need for a fundamental shift in our approach to the resolution of conflicts.[30]

In the context of global affairs, de Bono suggests that a third party can help resolve conflicts, a person skilled in creative problem solving using lateral thinking (or what de Bono has elsewhere defined as Po thinking) to *design* a new scenario.[31] de Bono takes advantage of an alternative mentioned earlier at the interpersonal level: for society to support those unable to resolve conflicts by themselves. de Bono does not use the same terms as Kegan, but his arguments are similar to the latter's description of the incapability of people using third-order ways of knowing to resolve issues that require fourth-order solutions.

Sustaining Equity and Pluralism in a Complex Society

The arguments of Kegan and de Bono cannot go uncontested, however. Whose views of conflict and its resolution are privileged by the assumptions about stages or orders of knowing espoused by Kegan and, indirectly, de Bono? For example, if, as Kegan suggests, a person's way of knowing is consistent across the various domains of life, perhaps there is more wisdom than first appears in the public's, or at least the media's, intense gaze into the personal lives of the rich and famous. Although the media rarely investigate these issues in depth, the ways the rich and famous frame their personal problems and deal with them may indeed indicate their "way of knowing" about public affairs as well. Nevertheless, newspaper, T.V., or radio producers who are themselves capable only of a third-order way of knowing cannot assist their audience in understanding a public figure's use of a fourth-order way of knowing. The significance of the data would be lost on the producers, and therefore that significance *would* not, and *could* not be made clear to the public. In this context, one might recall the outrage of many people when President Jimmy Carter admitted that he had, during his lifetime, "lusted in his heart" for a woman other than his wife. That he and his wife had found a way of knowing that reconciled that fact with their ongoing commitment to one another was beside the point for those people who found the two ideas irreconcilable, perhaps because they themselves were not fourth-order knowers.

This example may be viewed differently, however, if one considers it from a political rather than a psychosocial perspective. Perhaps a fourth-order solution—if that is indeed the order of knowing that brought the spouses to a resolution of the problem—was one that favored the male spouse and disfavored the female, since the female, having been slighted, was now asked to forgive the male, a situation familiar to women in every generation. In the context of the disparate power between men and women in our society, whose version of reality is privileged in this instance by Kegan's theory? The male's. While we cannot generalize in other instances from this example, it suggests that the political and social ramifications of Kegan's theory may be more controversial than he leads us to believe.

Just as we are unwilling to believe that a society might face revolution because the mental demands on the population had become intolerable for the majority, so also are we loath to admit that the hierarchy of ways of knowing—devised by psychologists to make normative statements about cognitive and affective development—might favor one group of people over another. Nevertheless, feminist critiques of developmental theories have shown that women have fared badly in relation to men according to the developmental hierarchies hypothesized by some male psychologists.[32] Kegan argues that there is a distinction, previously ignored, between subject-object theory (which posits the development of a person's ability to stand apart from situations and perceive them as objects separate from him- or herself: the basis of Kegan's orders of knowing) and relational theory (which provides one with voices of connectedness and separation). According to Kegan's latest analysis, a person can use either the voice of connectedness or that of separation at each order of knowing.[33] Thus, he maintains the validity of normative judgments within his own theoretical framework while showing how feminist differentiations of style and voice can be used to ensure gender (and race) equity in the application of his hierarchical theory.

People's level of personality development and their order of consciousness in relation to their reference group orientation is extraordinarily complex. In *Shades of Black: Diversity in African-American Identity*, William E. Cross, Jr. describes the five-stage process of nigrescence, a *resocializing* experience which "seeks to transform a preexisting identity (a non-Afrocentric identity) into one that is Afrocentric."[34] I have found it useful to juxtapose his theory, Kegan's, and de Bono's, in considering the issue of whether society is placing new, and frustrating, intellectual demands upon people. People at the third stage of nigrescence, Cross claims, go through a process of Immersion so intense that he speaks of them as "converts," with all the commitment, enthusiasm, and lack of confidence in their new identity that converts to any faith experience. The propensity to label and pass judgement on others, and to conform studiously with the norms of the new group, are signs of the third stage of nigrescence. At the fourth, Internalization, stage, these needs have subsided. Key markers of the Internalization stage are a shift away from other people's standards to a confidence in one's "personal standards of Blackness; from uncontrolled rage toward white people to controlled anger at oppressive systems and racist institutions. . . . "[35] There is a similarity here between Cross's fourth stage of nigrescence and Kegan's fourth order of consciousness. In Cross's analysis, one has moved "from a frame of reference where race and culture had low salience [the first, Pre-encounter stage] to a perspective that places high salience on Blackness in everyday life. With this change in salience comes membership in new organizations and changes in one's social network. . . . These changes define what is important in adult life, which is why the person feels totally new. Left unnoticed is the fact that his or her basic personality profile is the same as it was during Pre-encounter."[36]

Cross claims that, while all people at the Internalization stage of nigrescence will place a high salience on race, the intensity of that salience will depend upon a person's ideology. This distinction is particularly important to understand in a society that values pluralism and equity. Supporters (and opponents) of pluralism and equity may have reached any stage of nigrescence or any order of consciousness. As Cross points out, there are African Americans at the Internalization stage of nigrescence who are *not* supporters of multculturalism. They hold either what he calls a *vulgar* nationalism (based upon a belief that Blacks and Whites "are biogenetically different with Blacks of 'superior' stock") or a *traditional* nationalism (based upon beliefs other than biogenetic ones).

Thus, ideology may be crucial in people's willingness (as opposed to their ability) to cooperate with, tolerate, or rebel against their social and political environment. A multicultural society, which sees its diversity as a strength to be built upon, will provide its citizens with opportunities to develop intergroup and interpersonal relationships and public forums for the open discussion and resolution of discriminatory practices.

The Link Between Citizenship and Space and Communications Technology

New communications technology has drawn citizens of all societies into closer proximity with each other. Through satellite and cable technology, many of us are regularly in contact with people in countries other than our own. Wars in distant lands, such as the former Yugoslavia, impact on both our economic and our personal relations. To be a valuable member of our society a person not only has to become aware of the role the United States plays on the world stage and the role of the United Nations, but also has to assess the impact of modern technologies on those roles. More than sixty years ago, before the advent of rocket-propelled satellites, nuclear weapons, or commercial television, Montessori wrote: "If man [and woman] has managed to overcome the force of gravity and to travel freely and swiftly in the air, what country will henceforth be able to insist on territorial rights to this or that part of the earth? What country will be able to claim exclusive rights over the gravity of the earth or the outer space beyond the earth's atmosphere? Who will have the exclusive claim to the long waves and the short waves, the invisible causes of a mysterious kind of communication that nonetheless transports the voice of man and the thoughts of all humanity through space?"[37]

How powerful television has become in transmitting "the thoughts of all humanity through space" may be illustrated by its influence in helping turn public opinion in the United States against the war in Viet Nam. In the early 1990s, television helped produce pressure on the United States government and on the United Nations to send troops to assist in stemming famine in Somalia and disease in the Rwandan refugee camps in Zaire.

Whatever the topic portrayed by the media, they could play an even more important role than they do in informing viewers, listeners, and readers of the context within which any event is located. Viewers, listeners, and readers could be more active than they are in learning about that context before demanding action. Learning about the context of events has become more complicated with the immediacy of the media and the demands by viewers, listeners, and readers for action. For example, on T.V. we catch a glimpse of a starving child at the moment of her death on another continent. We express our horror and outrage by a telephone call to our congressman or woman, or to the White House. Why don't we stop this? Before we call, we may not query the motives of the producer who chose that particular site to film or the motives of the camera person who chose to focus on that particular child at that particular moment. We may not query the implication of the actions we then plead for. For example, we may ignore those in need whom we do not see portrayed on television, such as the homeless in our own city, even while we plead for assistance to the homeless we have seen in another country. The emotional impact of the visual image draws us into any drama we witness, but we get little guidance on how to interpret what we see, and how to evaluate its significance among the myriad of problems, at home and abroad, that cry out for our attention. Tomorrow's valuable citizen will need to both interpret and evaluate the significance of the images presented by the media.

This brings us back full circle to the ideas of Dewey and Montessori quoted earlier, for how we order our priorities depends on our sense of location and of self-in-relationship. Whoever's terminology we use, the task at hand is to facilitate people's learning so that they reflect about their location and their self-in-relationship-to-others in a world of diverse peoples linked by satellite and fiber-optic technology. To expand on the ideas described above, we should consider the issues of location and self-in-relationship in light of Nel Noddings's centers of care: "care for self, for intimate others, for associates and acquaintances, for distant others, for nonhuman animals, for plants and the physical environment, for the human-made world of objects and instruments, and for ideas."[38] Noddings makes a case for focusing the school curriculum on these centers of care to give students and teachers what Tom Mauhs-Pugh describes elsewhere in this volume as "robust concepts of consensus in determining the school's ethos." In this connection, the work of psychologists on small group interactions helps us facilitate people's sense of belonging. Though the connection between a person's successful participation in short-term communities and in a long-term community still has to be explored, there is reason to expect that such a connection exists. Indeed, successful long-term communities provide an ongoing series of short-term projects for their members to be involved in. It is likely that the most committed members of a long-term community regularly participate in short-term projects. Can we verify that the most committed members were those who had experienced positive feedback from participation in a short-term community *at a young age?* For example, those who serve on a political campaign in their youth may be more concerned with being active voters throughout their life than those who have not. In an electronic environment, the nature of short-term and long-term community projects must be different, but this thesis about commitment may remain intact.

How do the new information technologies affect people's ways of thinking and acting? Let us look at the issues of location and self-in-relationship. The very centers of care identified by Noddings may change in character as the interactions within and among them take place in a new media environment. For example, if I were a third grade child, my definition of who were my associates and my acquaintances might be very different if my school were networked with other schools in Europe, Asia, and Africa for social studies than if my school were not so networked. We still have to explore both the effect of the new media on people's understanding of loyalty, and their influence on people's desire for political and social action. We also have to explore the effect of the new media on our society's, and the world's, organizations and institutions. "The paradox of our time is that we have to respond to technologies we do not yet fully understand, whose implications we only faintly grasp, whose long term effects we can only surmise, and to do this, we have to use a vocabulary and an institutional structure fashioned, in its turn, as a response to a technological revolution that took place nearly two hundred years ago."[39]

The Challenge: To Maintain Pluralism and Equity in a Complex, Technological Society

Recent information technologies have increased the number of people who can communicate personally with others throughout the world, the density of the information that can be transferred, and the complexity of the exchanges that take place. In each of these cases, power, whether between teacher and taught or among individuals as a result of age, gender, race, or class, influences the information communicated, the form of the interaction, and the nature of the learning of the participants. In our society, where the drive to maintain both pluralism and equity is strong, these issues of power have to be raised to assess their influence on learning. Some of these relationships may become attenuated when an interaction takes place, not in person, but over an electronic network. For example, in an electronic environment that does not rely on video, new forms of power become apparent, while old forms, based on visual clues, disappear.[40]

A technology may be constrained, not only by the structure of a society's institutions, but also by the values of the society's members. For example, in our society, where equity is valued, people are concerned that access to networked computer-video machines is not available to all. Those with enough money may buy a computer with communication capability for their home. Others have access to such a machine at work, though not all workplaces have such machines. Many people can neither afford their own machine nor have access to one in the workplace. This limitation causes new inequities, and, in some cases, exacerbates existing inequities based on socio-economic status, race, and gender. This effect of the technology runs counter to the value of maintaining an equitable society. We have to ask ourselves, therefore, whether we are prepared to make laws to limit a specific technology to maintain equity. Or are there other mechanisms for maintaining equity that we can use? Can we (and should we if we can) constrain the technology in other ways? Can we suggest new applications for the technology that might eliminate other inequities? If we take no action, the new inequities will have lasting effects on the children of today and the adults of tomorrow.

The problem of new inequities is sometimes offset by the elimination of existing inequities: for example, the use of computer technology to facilitate communication for people with Down syndrome and autism. This development has been lauded for breaking down barriers that formerly caused inequities for people suffering from certain communication disabilities.

The need to maintain pluralism and equity has to be considered not only with regard to technology. Within the larger discussion about the complexity of life, pluralism and equity are important components. In a recent discussion about the purposes of schooling, the authors sought to explicate the complexity of knowing and learning. "In effect," they wrote, "the teacher, the students, and the various forms of knowledge are, as Michael Oakshott has observed, 'voices in a conversation, a conversation to which they each contribute in a distinctive way'. . . . [The conversation] leads students and teachers into possible worlds, to alternative views, and into a plurality of ways of understanding and making meaning."[41] Education as such a form of conversation privileges pluralism and equity in ways that lead to new methods of teaching and learning, where the teacher becomes also a learner, and where the learner becomes both a critic and teacher.

Conclusion

These complex ways of understanding the learning process, and what Kegan describes as the curriculum of life, demand from each of us an order of consciousness that is sophisticated indeed. In this chapter, we have examined how complexity in our lives arises from a confluence of forces that includes the mental demands placed upon us, the information technologies we use, and the concepts of pluralism and equity we value. Complexity inheres, not only in the individual's interpretations of reality, but in the structures of the society in which the individual exists. How far we can simplify the structures of our own society without damaging its fundamental values is open to question. As described above, we hold that "all citizens are entitled to the skills necessary for thoughtful and active citizenship," which means that society is obliged to provide the opportunity for every person to acquire those skills. While "equality does not require that everyone learn exactly the same things in exactly the same ways," it does require that any differences among people "not be used to diminish opportunities to learn or to gain access to knowledge."[42] Kegan suggests that we now demand of individuals a way of knowing, or an order of consciousness, more complex than has ever been demanded of people before. His solution is for us to pay attention to the curriculum of life, and to arrange, where feasible, for a dovetailing of experiences across life's domains so that we facilitate a person's progression from the third order to a fourth and even to a fifth order of consciousness.

I have suggested here that Kegan's analysis is useful for the education of tomorrow's valuable citizen. Nevertheless, I challenge its emphasis on the role of individual development as a solution to the complexities of life in a postindustrial environment. The structures of society are, after all, designed by individuals, who can choose which other individuals or groups to privilege and which to ignore or oppress. One could argue, with some justification I suspect, that the successful struggle for hegemony by the intellectual and professional middle class in England during the nineteenth century, manifested in new requirements for credentials based upon the results of school and university examinations,[43] was comparable to the successful struggle for hegemony by college and university educated professionals in the United States in the late twentieth century, manifested in the complexity of language and of ways of knowing needed to succeed in one's personal as well as one's work life. Each was constructed, by a group eager to assert its power, with claims that the new structures provided greater equity and met the needs of a changing society. In nineteenth-century England, the professional middle class succeeded in making the changes it had instituted to sustain its own power in society

seem to all the other members of society to be inevitable and necessary. It remains to be seen whether college- and university-
educated professionals in the United States will be able to persuade
all the other members of our society today of the necessity for the
complexity they posit, or whether this "creative minority," as Toynbee
might have called it, will find itself unable to attract the willing
assent of its fellows. If, indeed, the task of educating people to
Kegan's fourth and fifth order of consciousness proves impossible,
or takes longer than people find tolerable, how will those who cannot cope respond to the growing frustrations they feel in their
lives? One response might be increased acts of violence throughout
society. A reaction to those acts of violence might be that those with
power would abrogate the rights of their fellow citizens who seem
unable to cope. In doing so, the powerful would abandon the values
of pluralism and equity we have striven to maintain. They might
thereby destroy all possibility of a true participatory democracy.

To protect us from such a catastrophe, I suggest two lines of
action. Each seeks to mitigate the complexities of contemporary
life. First, we need to formulate the outcomes expected of people at
each stage, as they proceed through what Kegan calls "the curriculum of life." We need to identify ways to facilitate people's growth,
whether informally at home, in the neighborhood, in the workplace, on the Internet, and through the media, or formally in any
of those settings or in an educational institution, therapist's office,
voluntary organization, or social service agency. Second, we need to
examine continually all the institutions our society has developed
or will develop, to simplify—and where possible standardize—their
functions, while maintaining our commitment to pluralism and
equity and to the goal of providing each individual with the skills
he or she needs to participate fully as a citizen in society.

NOTES

1. The quotations in this paragraph are from David A. Hollinger,
"How Wide the Circle of the 'We'? American Intellectuals and the Problem
of the Ethnos since World War II," *American Historical Review* 98, no. 2
(April 1993): 317–37.

2. *Ibid.*: 332. In this section of his article, Hollinger describes the characteristics of what he calls "a postethnic perspective."

3. See, *Ibid.*, p. 229 ff.

4. Andrew Oldenquist, "Loyalties," *The Journal of Philosophy* 79, no. 4 (April 1982): 173–93. The quotation is from p. 181.

5. Maria Montessori, *Education and Peace* (Oxford: Clio Press Ltd., 1992), p. 23. From an address delivered in 1932 at the International Office of Education in Geneva, Switzerland.

6. *Ibid.*, p. 56. From an address entitled "The Form Education Must Take to be Able to Help the World in our Present Circumstances," delivered in 1937 at the Sixth International Montessori Congress in Copenhagen, Denmark.

7. John Dewey, *Moral Principles in Education* (New York: Philosophical Library, Inc., 1959), p. 11. [First published in 1909 as one of the Riverside Educational Monographs.]

8. For a discussion of these issues see Henry Giroux and Paulo Freire, "Introduction," in *Women Teaching for Change: Gender, Class and Power*, Kathleen Weiler, ed., (New York: Bergin and Garvey Publishers, 1988), pp. ix–xiv.

9. Marshall McLuhan, *Global Village: Transformation in World Life and Media in the Twenty-First Century* (New York: Oxford University Press, 1989).

10. Marshall McLuhan, *The Medium is the Massage* (New York: Random House, 1967).

11. See Edward Gibbon, *The Decline and Fall of the Roman Empire* (London: W. Strahan & T. Cadell, 1776); and Arnold J. Toynbee, *A Study of History*, vols. I–III (1934); vols. IV–VI (1939). Toynbee's fame in the United States was established with the publication of *A Study of History. Abridgement of Vols. I–VI* by D. C. Somervell (Oxford: Oxford University Press, 1946).

12. Marvin Lazerson, Judith Block McLaughlin, Bruce McPherson, and Stephen K. Bailey, *An Education of Value: The Purposes and Practices of Schools* (Cambridge: Cambridge University Press, 1985), p. xiii.

13. William H. McNeill, *Arnold Toynbee, a Life* (New York: Oxford University Press, 1989), pp. 159–60.

14. See Robert Kegan, *In Over Our Heads: The Mental Demands of Modern Life* (Cambridge: Harvard University Press, 1994).

15. *Ibid.*, p. 92.

16. *Ibid.*, pp. 305–34.

17. *Ibid.*, p. 37.

18. *Ibid*, p. 196.

19. See, for example, Marcia Mentkowski and Glen Rogers, "Connecting Education, Work, and Citizenship: How Assessment Can Help," *Metropolitan Universities* 4, no. 1 (Summer 1993): 34–46. Other longitudinal studies that could provide insights into the complexities of people's ways of knowing are summarized in Kathleen Day Hulbert and Diane Tickton Schuster, eds., *Women's Lives Through Time: Educated American Women of the Twentieth Century* (San Francisco: Jossey-Bass Publishers, 1993).

20. See Shoshana Zuboff, *In the Age of the Smart Machine: The Future of Work and Power* (New York: Basic Books, Inc., 1984), Chapter 2: "The Abstraction of Industrial Work." The quotation is from p.93.

21. *Ibid.*, p. 71.

22. *Ibid.*, p. 104.

23. *Ibid.*, p. 105.

24. See Edward de Bono, *The Use of Lateral Thinking* (London: Penguin Books, Ltd., 1990. Originally published in 1967.) And de Bono, *Conflicts: A Better Way to Resolve Them* (London: Penguin Books Ltd., 1991. First published in 1985.)

25. See Kegan, *In Over Our Heads*, pp. 53–70.

26. See Robert Bellah, Richard Madsen, William Sullivan, Ann Swidler, and Steven Tipton, *Habits of the Heart* (Berkeley: University of California Press, 1985).

27. Donald Schön, *The Reflective Practitioner* (New York: Basic Books, 1983), pp. 277–83.

28. For the role of psychoanalysis in influencing homemakers' perceptions of the sources of their discontent, see, Betty Friedan, *The Feminine Mystique* (New York: Norton, 1963).

29. See de Bono, *The Use of Lateral Thinking*.

30. de Bono, *Conflicts: A Better Way to Resolve Them*, p. viii.

31. See Edward de Bono, *Po: Beyond Yes and No* (London: Penguin Books, 1990. Originally published in 1972.)

32. See Carol Gilligan, *In a Different Voice* (Cambridge: Harvard University Press, 1982), and Mary Field Belenky, Blythe McVicker Clinchy, Nancy Rule Goldberger, and Jill Mattuck Tarule, *Women's Ways of Knowing: The Development of Self, Voice, and Mind* (New York: Basic Books, Inc., 1986).

33. Kegan, *In Over Our Heads*, pp. 198–233.

34. William E. Cross, Jr., *Shades of Black: Diversity in African-American Identity* (Philadelphia, Temple University Press, 1991), p. 190.

35. *Ibid.*, p. 210.

36. *Ibid.*, p. 212.

37. Montessori, *Education and Peace*, pp. 21–22. From an address delivered in 1932 at the International Office of Education in Geneva, Switzerland.

38. Nel Noddings, *The Challenge to Care in Schools: An Alternative Approach to Education* (New York: Teachers College Press, 1992), p. xiii. For an earlier and broader exploration of her ideas, see, also, Nel Noddings, *Caring: A Feminine Approach to Ethics and Moral Education* (Berkeley: University of California Press, 1984).

39. Joan N. Burstyn, "The Challenge to Education from New Technology," in *Preparation for Life? The Paradox of Education in the Late Twentieth Century*, Joan N. Burstyn, ed., (Philadelphia: Falmer Press, 1986), pp. 192–93.

40. For discussions of some of the issues raised here, see Robin P. Peek and Joan N. Burstyn, "In Pursuit of Improved Scholarly Communications," in *Desktop Publishing and the University*, Joan N. Burstyn, ed. (Syracuse: Syracuse University School of Education, 1991), and Joan N. Burstyn, " 'Who Benefits and Who Suffers': Gender and Education at the Dawn of the Age of Information Technology," in *Gender and Education*, Sari Knopp Biklen and Diane Pollard, eds., (Chicago: National Society for the Study of Education, 1993), pp. 107–25.

41. Lazerson, McLaughlin, McPherson, and Bailey, *An Education of Value*, p. 73.

42. *Ibid.*, p. xiii.

43. See Harold Perkin, *The Origins of Modern English Society, 1780–1880* (London: 1969).

Chapter 11

*"The end
is where we start from . . . "*

"The end is where we start from..."

T. S. Eliot, "Little Gidding"

This book began curiously. After the 1991 annual meeting of the American Educational Research Association in Chicago, six doctoral students from Syracuse University began a lively argument on the fourteen-hour drive home. They tried, unsuccessfully, to reach consensus on how to educate a valuable citizen of a valuable society. Eager to continue the argument, they began to engage the faculty and their student colleagues in the issue. The original group then decided to present a panel of short papers on the topic at national meetings in 1992. They met regularly to prepare their ideas, sharing them with groups within the university. Their panel was accepted for the annual meetings of both the American Educational Studies Association and the American Educational Research Association.

At those meetings, audiences of scholars from around the country joined in lively discussion. At the end, we began a new phase of the project. By this time, "we" included myself and my colleague, Emily Robertson, a philosopher of education who constantly shared her wisdom with us, even though her commitments precluded her writing a chapter for this book. Michelle Maher and Cheryl Billings, active in the original discussions and as panelists, participated only briefly in the next phase. We expanded the group, however, by inviting James and Ellen Giarelli, Barbara McEwan, Mary Stanley, and Donald Warren to join the discussion and contribute essays to this book. Our goal, as we wrote to them, was to create "a collaborative, educational tool which could stand as an innovative model for its process, content, and form. We believe such a cooperative effort as this will continue to help transcend traditional boundaries and barriers between atomized students, between students and professors, and between scholars from different universities."

For us, the process of creating this book has been as important as its completion. Scholars from a variety of backgrounds have engaged in our discussion. We have shared our ideas as widely as possible. The process has taken time—more time than I envisioned when I agreed to edit the book—but it has been generative.

So here we are at the end. Have we answered the question: how should we educate people to become valuable members of tomorrow's society? Not directly. We have clarified what that question means. And we have provided guidance for action. Several authors in the book are scholar-practitioners, working with schools, teachers, and community groups. There is a synergy between our ideas and actions.

If we take T. S. Eliot's aphorism seriously, where do we go from here? You who have read our thoughts, listened vicariously to our discussions by reading this book, what do you think? We could develop a new and larger discussion group, on the Internet, perhaps, or through small teleconferences. We could augment the synergy between our ideas and actions by planning a network of educational innovations. The shape of any new beginning depends upon the wishes of the group, of those who choose to become part of a new "we." David Hollinger suggests that we should stretch the circle of the "we" as far as possible. The authors of this book would like to do that.

Any future development depends upon the innovative methods that we—the readership of this book—dream up to expand the conversation and to share our experiences. "The end is where we start from . . . "

CONTRIBUTORS

Joan N. Burstyn, editor, is Professor of Cultural Foundations of Education and of History, Syracuse University.

John Covaleskie is Assistant Professor of Education, Northern Michigan University.

James M. Giarelli is Associate Professor in the Graduate School of Education, Rutgers, the State University of New Jersey.

Ellen Giarelli is Adjunct Faculty in the Graduate School of Education and Human Services, Seton Hall University.

Jerilyn Fay Kelle is a doctoral student in Cultural Foundations of Education, Syracuse University.

Thomas Mauhs-Pugh is Visiting Assistant Professor, Department of Education, Dartmouth College.

Barbara McEwan is Assistant Professor, Elementary Education, School of Education, College of Home Economics and Education, Oregon State University.

Mary B. Stanley is Associate Professor of Public Affairs, the Maxwell School, Syracuse University.

Donald Warren is University Dean and Professor of Education, School of Education, Indiana University.

Zeus Yiamouyiannis is a doctoral student in Cultural Foundations of Education, Syracuse University.

INDEX

Compiled by Hannah M. King

The alphabetical arrangement is word by word.
Added to the page number, n indicates a chapter endnote.
Chapter endnotes are indexed to the citing page and to the note if the note
  includes comments.
Titles are alphabetized under the first significant word.
Article titles are enclosed in quotes and book and journal titles are italicized.